Praise for
Understanding Human Nature

Richard's book really brought home to me the importance of truly getting to know ourselves as human beings – of learning to listen to and trust the quiet whispers of the heart, which can often be drowned out by the voices of those around us, as well as by our own inner critic.

Expertise is only valuable if the expert can help other people to understand it without their huge training and experience. Albert Einstein once said, "If you can't explain it to a six-year-old, you don't understand it yourself." Richard's clarity of explanation backed up by practical tips and exercises clearly shows a deep understanding of esoteric concepts such as soul, chakras, subtle energy, vibrations, yin and yang and the five elements that are often explained in complicated terms. In this book, Richard has 'nailed it' by clearly explaining these somewhat complicated concepts so that those of us without his vast experience and expertise can understand these concepts and enhance our lives as we learn to get closer to our true selves and live a more balanced and satisfying life. Life is precious and when we can learn to trust and follow our own hearts, and do what we love, we can truly be in our 'element'.

Thank you Richard for your timely and much needed messages of hope and positivity in a sometimes negative world.

Mary Dalgleish, Therapist, Teacher, Author,
Vice President - Federation of Holistic Therapists (FHT)

In this "Instruction Manual", Richard uses his personal experiences and insights as a starting point, enabling you to investigate the intricate and marvellous landscape of human nature. His practical, step-by-step explanations help make the ideas accessible and easy to follow. The "nuts and bolts" sections and exercises he includes help to keep the ideas grounded and enable you to put these ideas into action. Although designed to be read cover to cover, it's quite useful, as Richard himself says, to dip in and out and focus on particular areas of interest. As with any instruction manual, you will find yourself returning to certain sections in order to broaden and deepen your understanding. Highly recommended.

Ken Shifrin, M.Ac., F.B.Ac.C., Master of Acupuncture, Fellow of the British Acupuncture Council

This book is unique; it is both complex and easy to read. Well thought-out, the content, drawn from many years of personal experience, extensive research and practical application, is presented in a consistent and accessible way with 'nuts and bolts tutorials' in each chapter to help the reader discover and maintain the inner and outer harmony of their journey through life.

I have known the author for 20 years and his commitment to seeking understanding of the nature of Energy has never faltered, even in times of extreme personal stress. I can recommend this book to all seekers as an abundant source of information and practical help.

Stella Longland, Sun Moon Dancer and Author

Richard's voice is unpretentious and creative. He brings a no-nonsense approach to that which is universal in us all, giving accessible exercises and relatable examples. This book will fit neatly on the shelf of any therapist or teacher, or absolutely anyone seeking to connect with their own soul wisdom.

Laura Parr, Yoga Teacher and Therapist

This insightful book explores the meaning of body-mind-spirit in a conversational and experiential way that engages the reader immediately. Richard Brook has given the background to many concepts of Chinese medicine, energy work and movement and suggests tasks and exercises for the individual to delve into and nourish their own holistic life with better understanding.

Richard Brook has created this "User's Guide to Life" for the curious reader wishing to explore their holistic body, mind and spirit. If you want to know more about the interconnectedness of human nature with the world, the universe, each other and ourselves, then read this book!

As an Amatsu Practitioner and teacher of anatomy, I feel this book is a refreshing balance of science, belief and the acknowledgement of that which we don't yet understand. It is a book for the curious, to entice the reader to observe and explore themselves, both within the confines of their body, and how it interrelates to their environment and each other.

Jane Langston, Co-Author of Muscle Testing: A Concise Guide

Reading "Understanding Human Nature" is a rich and satisfying experience. Richard offers an explorative guide on how to be a fully present and embodied being. He shows a clear and integrative path towards feeling "at home" within our own body and establishing connections within ourselves and with others in the world.

Christina Argyropoulou, Movement Therapist

This book successfully brings together key elements from a variety of different healing systems and traditions. For anyone seeking to deepen their relationship with the inner-self, navigate the hectic modern world, and find their true calling in life... This is possibly the most important user's guide you will ever read.

Natalie Chandra Saunders LicAc, Author of The Qi of Tea

Understanding Human Nature:

A User's Guide to Life

The one instruction manual you really do need to read

RICHARD BROOK

Matador
9 Priory Business Park,
Wistow Road, Kibworth Beauchamp,
Leicestershire. LE8 0RX
Tel: 0116 279 2299
Email: books@troubador.co.uk
Web: www.troubador.co.uk/matador
Twitter: @matadorbooks

ISBN 978 1800461 680

British Library Cataloguing in Publication Data.
A catalogue record for this book is available from the British Library.

Printed and bound by CPI Group (UK) Ltd, Croydon, CR0 4YY
Typeset in 12pt Minion Pro by Troubador Publishing Ltd, Leicester, UK

Matador is an imprint of Troubador Publishing Ltd

Family

Contents

Contents

Contents

Acknowledgements

This epic undertaking (well epic for me!) wouldn't have been possible without support from many quarters and my own opportunities to learn from many great teachers! Firstly, taking the broad perspective I have to thank the biggest teacher of them all – life, and the life journey I've had. Ultimately the gifts and curveballs that life throws at you, outside of any kind of 'intentional' education or classroom, mean it is simply an unceasing learning experience in itself (you can't help but be tutored by the events that happen to you!). It's the ultimate on-the-job training and I appreciate mine – the harmony and the struggles – as all part of helping me sharpen and fine-tune my sense of purpose and ability to do life better!

Firstly, a massive thanks to my family who have always supported me; I couldn't have asked for a better home life in my formative years.

I've also been absolutely blessed to have had some amazing teachers and mentors over the years that I wish to acknowledge. Some I've had lots of contact with, others not so much, but the common denominator is that their essence has sat as a guiding force on my shoulder over the years for which I'm grateful. Firstly, take a bow John Wilson, who as my tai chi instructor at university was my first real guiding light in the holistic world. While John helped me explore previously uncharted territory, the power of his teaching, to me, was utterly grounding, as he taught me it was ok to still be yourself and be 'spiritual' at the same time. He shattered the ideal I had at that young age of *'trying'* to be spiritual as his acceptance of his own human attributes (warts and all) and cultural idiosyncrasies was a breath of fresh air while I was spending so much time trying to suppress my own. John also introduced me to ceremonial practices, such as Sun Moon Dances which have been a massive influence in my personal growth.

Next up, Ken Shifrin, who was dean at the College of Traditional Acupuncture, has also helped me immeasurably over the years, often when I've been at my most discombobulated and lost. His steady hand, assured presence, rock-like support and incredibly perceptive wisdom about the 5 Elements helped provide me with inspiration and a map to get back on track and to this day helps to keep me there!

Third on my hall of fame is Ya'Acov Darling Khan, co-founder of the School of Movement Medicine with his wife Susannah who prior to that had an 18-year apprenticeship to Gabrielle Roth, representing the 5Rhythms in Europe. Although I had much less contact time with Ya'Acov than a lot of my other teachers and mentors, he showed me that a gentle presence can actually be a fiercely strong presence that can touch people right down to their core. This was a wonderful contrast from the toxic masculinity more aligned with 'overpowering' others that I often witnessed in my youth.

Of my yoga teachers I want to thank Ruth Boaler, Joshna Patel, Anoushka Dack and all at Dru Yoga for introducing me to a heartfelt practice that touches me as much today as it did the first time I ever practised. I enjoyed the first class I attended so much that I stayed on my mat and did the class that immediately followed it too! From my time in Portugal I have to thank Tania Surya at Alma Sana in Portimao. Tania is the most naturally creative yoga teacher I've ever had the privilege to practise with and I'm tremendously grateful for her ability to connect me with my own deep feminine, the intuitive wisdom and capacity to nurture my own body. I've never become a yoga class regular because I *think* it's something I should attend (it has to run deeper than that for me); it has to be a place where my heart can relax and I can drop whatever stress I'm walking into the room with and connect to my own inner voice. Now that's what I call yoga and all these teachers have brought me that gift.

From my dance and movement teachers, huge appreciation to Dawn Morgan for the seven years of 5Rhythms classes while I lived back in the Midlands, and all the London teachers for providing the possibility of dancing every day of the week and shaking off the city – amazing! To Susannah Darling Khan for the year-long 5Rhythms ongoing group where I really had the chance to dissect and understand how the rhythms inhabit our lives, as well as the dance floor.

To the beautiful people who are involved with the organisation of the UK Sun Moon and Drum Dances, particularly Stella Longland and Ocean Graham. Arranging for a group of people to dance for three days while dry fasting takes not only organisational skills but also a huge depth of understanding of life dynamics and strong trust and faith in what you feel creatively inclined to do.

I've had the privilege of being the recipient of many great treatments over the years and wish to give special thanks to Clive Lindley-Jones and Trixie Denneborg for helping keep me in one piece.

At the wonderful Moinhos Velhos retreat in the Algarve where I spend so much time, huge thanks to the late Frank Jensen, late Anne Karine Moss, Janni Jensen, Ed van Tegelen, Debby van Tegelen-Cremers, Karen de Mey and Chris Lloyd Pack for helping me have a place to live where for the first time in many, many years I actually felt at home. What a journey I've had with that place and long may it continue.

Related to writing this book, I wish to give a huge thanks to Chris and Karen for providing me with the perfect location to write the vast majority of this book and let my creative inspiration flow. I loved those four months tucked away in the caravan in the Algarve! Similar thanks too for the retreat spaces of Didier Calado and Wim Molinello where I also did big chunks of writing! Also I have to thank Frances Coles and Anu Sildnik for their help in turning the images in my head into fantastic illustrations and charts, Karen Williams for her book mentoring, Louise Lubke Cuss for her editing skills and the team at Matador.

To my close friends who've given me the space to just be me and spill out my heart: Michael Arnold who always had time for me, I honestly don't know how he did it; ditto Verity Mitchell, what a golden heart she has. Vernon James and Vanessa Pitt for being a part of my Creative Yoga London tribe, experiences which have bound us together to this day. Liliana Cunha, Fatima Fernandes, Tom Allen, Gabriela Arbesova and Stefanie Joyce who have been superstars during my time in Portugal and France.

Prologue

No more press-ups on the pavement at midnight

There have been many turning points in my life. Some big. Some dramatic. And some seemingly imperceptible at the time, until I look back and realise how much they inform who I am today. It's all too easy to call them low points, when in reality they are just 'turning points', navigational aids, letting me know I'm diverting off track or have some work to do.

I've always been interested in finding out how things work. Not inanimate objects, but how life itself works. Sure, at school, we are taught concepts, but these mainly lend themselves towards making one 'successful' within the confines and perspective of a particular society, rather than teaching you about the whole game of life. Where on earth – literally! – was any kind of narrative, explanation or instruction manual on life itself?

Now I get that we are all different. My brother's bliss, his 'Tao', path and purpose, is tinkering with his 500cc Ducati. He's happy stripping it down and rebuilding its engines, whereas my purpose is very different. It took me years to work out that we all have our own destiny and bliss. There's no judgement; it is what it is! I spent years wondering why I wasn't the same as seemingly everyone around me, until I found my place.

Let's go back to one of my turning points. I was about 17. My parents had separated which catalysed some big changes for me and a collapse of sorts. I don't attribute any blame or fault whatsoever, as like most parents they were trying as hard as they could, and I had a good childhood. Even if you perceive your parents' behaviour to be misaligned, keeping the broader holistic perspective, they are not the only significant input to shape you into who you are today. They are just two people in a long line of ancestral nuances passed down from generation to generation.

They also might not have known any better in terms of their own behaviour, having had narrow terms of reference of 'how to live' themselves. So while they help to give you genetic form, and some tendencies, it's not their sole 'fault' who you turn out to be.

In fact, blaming anyone else takes away our own power to change – and our parents tend to be an easy and favourite target! So I like to be quick to jump in when I share an idea that could inadvertently give you the ammunition to disempower yourself, and instead make sure you rethink the perspective away from all the new age and self-help baggage commonly associated with those ideas.

I'm also influenced by a Native American belief that you actually choose your own parents. Yes, you heard it right: before being conceived, you hang out as a soul before choosing the parents who have the right 'vibration' and essence for your soul growth and challenges. Try reflecting on that next time you choose to blame your folks for something!

Anyway, I digress. I was 17, my parents had split a couple of years previously and until then I had been nicely cocooned in a family and somewhat sheltered, which meant I never really had to reach out to seek or find answers. So ultimately, looking back now, their separation, although a source of pain, was the catalyst for me being who I am today. It forced me to go out and explore the world, and for that I am grateful.

One of the consequences of this significant rupture of my cocoon was that *in my mind*, on some kind of *logical* level, I wanted to almost adopt the group of friends I'd now buddied up with as my 'new' family and 'secure unit'. (Yes, I'm sure that you can see this intriguing double meaning of 'secure unit'!)

The unexpected collapse of familial comfort had a massive impact on me as the security and solidity it represented, which I know now as my 'Earth Element' in Chinese medicine, had crumbled away. I was hurting and I didn't know how to handle it all. Looking back, I wonder, what was I *thinking*? How could I do a like-for-like replacement of my family with another group of people?

So I ran to my mind, rather than my feelings, throwing lots of energy into these new relationships. And it was fun to some degree. I was a teenager with lots of energy reaching out, as you do at that age, seeking an identity, but I didn't know myself, let alone these new people I'd only recently met!

I adopted the favoured demeanour of the livewire zany one. It made others laugh and helped me feel included and significant. This was a complete contrast to the studious intellectual person I was at school. But with the parental 'earthquake' that previous self-identity had gone out the window, and I'd also discovered drinking, not only as a social lubricant, but also as a means to be 'in' with my new friends.

I also had my first real girlfriend at this point, again a relationship I was totally ill at ease with handling. I was already a leaning tower of Pisa trying to reach out via this zany drunken personality that I had embraced over my sensitive, subtle depths, but the depths were becoming dangerously discordant, full of unprocessed emotion, and now here I was trying to manage my first true reciprocated love.

One night we all met round my friend's house, and I remember feeling deeply uncomfortable inside, struggling to keep up with the energy and effort needed to slip into my caricature zany character when there was so much inner distress. And there was more beer to drink. Did I really want to drink more beer? Not really; I wasn't brought up to drink, and while I could go through periods of it to participate with the group around me, the constant nature of it wasn't what I wanted.

I was distressed. The weight of expectation *'in my mind'* to be all the things I just didn't FEEL like being was heavy. That night I was overthinking like crazy, self-analysing why I couldn't slip into the spontaneous zany character and feeling very beleaguered inside. I couldn't understand the secret of why sometimes I could be the carefree crazy zany one and then at other times be so lost in the darkness – sometimes I would actually 'snap' quite suddenly back into the present moment from these heavy thought-ridden states but *'I'* didn't know what to do to make it happen.

While my friends partied inside the house, I took myself outside to try and snap myself out of it. I actually started doing press-ups outside on the pavement. Bizarre, I know, but somehow I associated doing exercise with something that could help, and in that moment, I was willing to try anything to ease my state.

Over time things became progressively more awkward with those friends – at least inside me, even if they weren't aware of it. I felt a sense of love and affinity through the experiences we'd had together, but on some level I never quite got past the feeling that I didn't quite belong and so I drifted away. I wanted the sense of comfort I had with my own family, but of course there was no going back.

Things became even more difficult with my girlfriend and my family, with some distressing and upsetting situations, even though everyone was trying. All I really remember now is falling down a deep depressive hole that lasted about four years, save for a few chinks of light when I started to discover holistic therapies and working in nature. The good thing about chinks of light is that they give you perspective and catalyse the mind to try and work out why some things work, and some things don't!

Looking back to that time, I had no clue what I was doing. I had no clue how life worked, no understanding of my own thoughts, feelings and emotions, no awareness of how to look after my body and certainly no clue about understanding what was going on in my mind or relationship dynamics. And as for learning a set of appropriate language, a narrative to explain my feelings, forget about it!

I now know that the constant 'pushing out' into my zany drunken character was me trying to force myself to be constantly 'yang' because I was deeply uncomfortable with retreating into the depths of my 'yin'. Yin is where we go inside and regenerate, clean ourselves up and make peace with our inner world. I didn't want to be in my inner world, as it was troubled, but there's a problem with this. Yin and yang naturally balance each other. It's a natural law, part of the matrix of life. And when you don't you become fatigued, and a few years later this became a big problem for me.

I was constantly in a state of 'mindfucking', as one of my teachers used to call it! At the tip of the iceberg of emotional unhappiness was my mind constantly trying to work things out. But trying to understand what my mind was actually trying to tell me about what I needed, forget about it! It was just like a giant argument going on in there. Fast forward to the present, and now I can perceive the subtlest shifts in my mental state and what it means on an emotional and lifestyle level, and help other people to do the same.

And as for the idea that behind all the painful chaos there was an actual intelligence at work – the intelligence of the soul, playing witness to what I was doing and trying to actually give me direction – well, forget about that too! It might have sounded like a nice idea if someone had been able to explain it to me, but I still would have had no clue how to actually access or interpret that part of me. These days tuning into that level of my being is a core aspect of my work.

I also had no perspective. Now I can see my parents' separation – amongst the sea of other experiences that can also be a source of pain – as actually a catalyst to make me explore life, to make me who I am today, and for that I'm grateful.

How I wish it could have been possible to give my younger self a copy of this book, as boy did I need a manual! In fact, I almost feel it borders on negligent that we are never actually given some kind of guide to help us understand our experience on Earth. It should be the first book we are given – how to live and be a human successfully.

We get a torrent of information aimed at teaching us the intellectual and manual skills designed to enable us to get 'good' jobs (good in the sense that they will make you money and feed the rat race, not feed your soul) but what about information about being a good, satisfied human being who understands life, not just how to make a quick penny? Where is that?

So my experiences stimulated me to become a life mechanic – to work out why some things work, and others don't. What are the nuts and bolts of the engine of my life and how do I get it in tune? As I see my brother fix his bike and speed off into the distance, this book offers you insights into helping to fix your understanding of life. Now see what you can do with that.

1

Introduction

There are so many spiritual, new age and natural health practices out there nowadays that we are trying to parachute into our modern-day lives. The result is this grinding juxtaposition of your Tuesday night yoga class, Wednesday night massage or week-long yoga retreat against the chaos and spiritual distress of your everyday life.

You might feel this clash as soon as you make the lonely commute home after the classes and events that actually do fill your heart, or during the social night out full of alcohol which barely scrapes the surface of what you really want to feel nourished. Or perhaps you feel it most when you wake up to another day in a concrete jungle overwhelmed with technology that's meant to help you connect with people – somewhat bizarre when in reality people barely feel comfortable raising a smile as they walk past you in the street.

Maybe it's when you wake up in the morning and drag yourself to another adrenalin-fuelled day at work as the pressure is on. Not the pressure for you to achieve what's deep in your *longing* soul, all the compacted dreams you've got stowed away in there from the day you were born, but simply the pressure to make money for 'someone' as you face the bleak reality that you're just another person in the rat race. Or maybe waking up to another day in a job you hate or just tolerate is all you have as you just don't know what else to do!

Possibly it strikes you most as you are rushing around frantically in the winter feeling exhausted to your bones, catching a glimpse out the corner of your eye at nature and the trees around you that are seemingly still, having a rest, but having no time to muse on that as you've got to keep pushing to get things done!

Perhaps it's when your backache or depression becomes so bad you finally go to the doctor's hoping for some kind of healing for the problem but instead walk out despairingly with another packet of painkillers or antidepressants?

Or is it when you end another relationship because it just doesn't match up to the Hollywood image of how it's meant to be?

What is going on?!

Nobody told you it was going to be like this, did they? These ideas were force-fed to you as being the norm from the day you were born and pushed even more as soon as you got into school: 'real life' they call it. And you were meant to fall for it, hook, line and sinker, and you once did, but the only problem now is that you've started to wake up.

The connection with your soul and natural life has been stoked by your engagement with these soulful natural practices such as yoga, dance, mindfulness and time spent in nature, and now there is no going back! You can try putting your head back into the sand after the bliss of your class or retreat, try getting back to the 'real life' you are meant to dutifully play out, but it's too late.

Whether you like it or not, you've been reborn into your own soul wisdom, the chance and opportunity to live out your birthright of who you actually are. It's time to close that gap between your bliss state when you do touch on the exalted territory of your heart and the rest of the f**king spiritually pitiful existence we have somehow contrived to create and become a diehard, authentic version of who you *actually* are. In all areas of your life!

It's time to be given the instruction manual to be yourself that you should have been given the day you were born, if only the people around you knew it existed, and probably weren't too bitter at the stress they had to endure in their own 'real life' to let you see it!

And here it is. Instead of filling your mind with ways to function in the 'real world' (which in fact is a crazy construct of Western civilisation which mostly pulls you away from everything that is naturally and actually important to you), here are the instructions to find who you are and how to function as a naturally exhilarated person in this reality and hack the system altogether!

Learn how to connect with your soul and interpret when it's whispering meaningful actions to take in your life, and how to feel it right now in your heart when you are doing something that's meaningful TO YOU.

Discover how you connect to the people and world around you, how you are bound together through the mechanics of vibration and resonance and why what you feel around a person or in a place has meaning, irrespective of what your logical mind tells you must be true.

Understand the natural energetic laws that are acting on your body-mind-spirit and directing the flow of your energy way more than the cultural demands of your society (and those of your boss) can ever contend with. Learn how these unceasing patterns of yin and yang and the Five Elements manifest in both your inner and outer world and how to be in tune with them – essential if you are going to live a vitally healthy life!

You'll find out how to observe and master how the inner terrain of your mind works and how it's just comprised of the same simple patterns as the rest of nature.

Explore relationship dynamics for what they truly are and dump the fantasies in favour of what is true and genuine.

And learn to understand, in depth, how healing practices such as yoga, meditation and Chinese medicine work and how they nourish your soul.

Reading this book will help you understand the importance of your life purpose and successfully managing both your internal physiology and the circumstances around you to nourish and provide the conditions for you to thrive. It will help you understand that abundant health is your soul sitting within your body and directing through the heart the other elements of you to give you what you need.

And you will be empowered! You will feel clear to change the circumstances around you when they aren't in alignment with your highest potential AND also have the capacity to work on yourself when you know the limiting factor is within. Wisdom and understanding is discerning which and knowing the difference!

I have often thought that the more you learn the better you should get at something; so your life should also be getting better as you develop. If your life isn't getting better, you might want to check you are absorbing the lessons life is sending your way or indeed, check you are learning the right stuff about life itself. And this is my attempt to share some wisdom that might help with that!

The book has been written to be read from cover to cover, but trust your instincts as well. If you are guided to dip in and out, then please do so. We are often working on certain aspects of our lives at a particular time and if something is more relevant now, trust your gut!

Understanding Human Nature brings together 25 years of my experiences in yoga and meditation (teaching and practising), acupuncture and Chinese medicine, dance and movement, retreat facilitation, ceremonies inspired by Native American mysticism, tantra and community living.

You'll learn from the countless hours I've spent treating acupuncture patients who lay bare to me what really matters; the hundreds of yoga classes I've taught helping people to reconnect to their body, heart and soul; the wisdom I've accumulated from participating in ceremonies (such as Sun Moon Dances where you dance for three days without food and water); the thousands of hours of conscious dance observing the instinctive wisdom of the body and group dynamics; my studies of tantric intimacy and understanding the mechanics of human relating, and my years spent living in intentional communities where life becomes about expressing your natural gifts to support the whole, not fitting in to make money! And finally the wisdom I've gleaned from simply learning to live my life from my heart.

Over that time I've been lucky enough to work in the grind of the busiest cities, like London, but also the most exquisitely beautiful natural settings, so I've got to see and understand both sides – that in the city you are always striving to achieve and *be* someone, whereas in nature, you already *are* someone!

And now it's time to be you.

2

Understanding the Human 'Energetic' Anatomy - the Soul

My soulful journey

If someone had mentioned to me years ago the idea that I had a soul it would have been just another 'idea' in my conceptual mind, another theory to file away. I believe the soul is something that you have to 'touch' inside, sometimes deep inside, and it was only initially through doing many 'embodied', 'spiritual' or 'soulful' practices such as Sun Moon Dances, 5Rhythms Dance, natural therapies and lots of yoga that I began to touch upon mine.

So what is the soul? Imagine a seed of light within you that has the capacity to expand and contract; this in essence is the soul. When the soul finds itself in a situation that engages it, doing something that you like, that seed of light expands and encompasses you and you are totally embodied within the radiance of it. It becomes your essence, your aura and charisma and spreads out in every direction around you, touching the life around you too.

However let me be clear here. The idea isn't just to be accessing your soul through intense or sometimes radical spiritual experiences outlined above – it's about getting your soul essence into every part of your life, every moment, as why would you ever want to be cut off from your own light? The practices I outline above are just ways to help you get connected again if you get cut off. The connection you feel in those practices acts as a template to remind you that you are more than a body and a brain, and then you bring that state of being off your yoga mat, off the dance floor, out of the therapy room or wherever and into your life!

In my late teens and early twenties, I had to dig really deep to find my soul, as I had become so disconnected at times. There were periods that were full of a darkness and emptiness, as I wasn't doing things to let my soul off its leash and fulfil my being. I recognise that sometimes there were huge gaps between the whispers of my soul and the limiting beliefs on the surface of my mind – perhaps those beliefs weren't allowing me to entertain the essence of what my soul desired, so I wasn't following its calling, or simply the circumstances around me hadn't really engaged with my soul itself.

In discovering my soul, I found a sense of peace and direction I'd never accessed before. I was finding my purpose, realising that I have a powerful healer living inside of me. And again, to be clear, that 'healer' doesn't have to be someone who does therapies for a living, it's just that when you find your soul, you become a healer even if you are digging holes for a living as long as that's your purpose! This is because you are bringing a healing quality to each moment of your existence.

In essence, we all have a calling, but with me it took some time for my conscious mind to come to terms with what my soul would be whispering! Growing up, being an acupuncturist or yoga teacher wasn't really on the list of occupations that you'd usually choose, so this is where some of the limiting beliefs can arise from. You either feel you have to move towards what society places a high value judgement on, or you simply don't have the context or awareness of what you might actually fit into. I didn't really give myself a sense of permission to do those things I was drawn to as I also had to contend with the projections and 'norms' from the people and culture around me which initially influenced me and my beliefs, until I garnered enough trust in who I am to just do what felt right for me.

It would be remiss of me here not to mention the role of my parents, close ones and societal norms. While my parents loved me to bits, they also had the potential, like most of us, to be limited by their existing 'terms of reference' for how they saw the world, and as mentioned being an acupuncturist or yoga teacher was not part of the back catalogue of occupations they would have projected onto me. Not because they were being malicious, but just because they wouldn't have known – their idea of a successful career would have more likely been an accountant or lawyer!

And as for encouraging the idea of going away for 10 days' intensive personal development work or doing yoga most days to 'find and connect with myself', well this was also hardly considered normal to those around me. To some degree, you have to unravel and separate the projections of others that you soak up into your own mind and work out who you actually are and become self-empowered.

So initially it felt a bit like trial and error, as I made the switch from what I call 'external navigation' to 'internal navigation'.

With external navigation we tend to make decisions based on the value judgements of the people around us and societal norms when making choices in life, whereas in internal navigation we are making choices that come from within. And over time I've increasingly moved to internal navigation; I get my answers within and act on them, and have very much narrowed the gap between soulless aspects of my life and peak experiences (such as the retreats and workshops) which were full of soul. Now every part of my life is touched by soul – or else what's the point? I cringe now when I hear family members proudly asserting what a great job a younger relative has because they are working for so-and-so and earning big money, even though the younger relative hates the job!

For more on internal and external navigation please visit this video blog: Internal v/s External Navigation[i]

As I've developed, sometimes I'm in situations where I feel like I'm living out my soul; it's so on the surface, it's like my entire being is a giant beating heart of what is important to me. Then life is easy. I don't have to 'think' or do intense practices to find my love and soul. I'm just happy as I'm in my essence.

I tend to feel completely soul embodied[1] when I'm doing acupuncture treatments, teaching yoga or giving workshops

---

i   www.creativewellness.co.uk/bookblogs

– it's as if all other internal chatter drops away out of my mind and I feel totally at 'One'[2]. For want of a better description it's as if I totally drop into my body and there is no longer any division between me and the world around me. When I'm doing something that I love so much there is no need to have any trepidation of the world around me; I'm in my 'element'.

A remarkable time for me is when I'm facilitating at Moinhos Velhos retreat in the Algarve. When I'm there I feel like my soul can just be so on the surface and met on so many levels. I do all the things that I love, offer loads of healing work, have great connections with people, community, professional development, fun, all in one place. Times like this can really help to shift your template and raise the bar of what you think is possible. Although we evolve and need change to keep the soul stimulated, don't ever dismiss times like these as simply being a 'holiday' or somehow not 'real life', which is something the naysayers will have you believe!

However, listening to the soul also isn't a one-hit wonder which always takes you towards the fun stuff; it's something you have to do often, and you have to find ways to constantly access it. Here's where your regular practices need to come in, so you don't lose track of what's inside and talking to you. Things evolve and sometimes we have to do what I think of as the 'long walk'.

The long walk is where the soul is seemingly asking to move on from a situation we have become *overly* comfortable with, or which is no longer feeding or nourishing us, since the soul prompts you when you aren't living fully as it likes to evolve and have new experiences. I've had this many times in my life.

My father passed on after an illness in 2003 and I went

back to live in his house towards the end of his life, which was a remarkable relief to me at the time, to be somewhere I felt comfortable and at ease, and just be with my dad. It completed something for me as when my parents had separated I lived with my mom, which was great, but I also just missed my dad, so going back there let me finish something I felt I'd missed.

However, I ended up staying way longer in his house than perhaps was for my greater good – about another seven years – as I didn't want to leave somewhere I'd finally felt so good after the difficulties of the preceding years! And that sense of flow was present for a long while, but then circumstances around me began to make it more and more difficult to stay there; finances became difficult, I had to have lodgers that created hassles and such like. The universe has a way of making things awkward when it's time to go as the situation is no longer in sync any more!

And I remember one day standing and looking out of the window at the field in front of his house, just as I had done at some point pretty much every day for seven years, and asking myself if I should stay or go. One part of me desperately wanted to cling on to what had been, and I was thinking of so many reasons to justify staying, but the thing is, I realised that by the time I was asking myself this question it was already too late as the situation was no longer fulfilling me. I was no longer immersed in it – you could say my soul was bored!

I remember many years ago a wise lady I met travelling around Canada, who said to me, "You don't have to justify something that fulfils you," and this was bang on the case here. I was trying to come up with all the reasons to stay, but it was too late. I'd chewed on that bone till there was nothing left.

So it's a bit like taking a long walk; sometimes you don't

know what's going to happen next, and the first part of the journey can be a bit arduous, but you don't know what riches are around the corner when you start moving!

Since the soul has a much broader 360-degree view on things and is connected to a much greater perspective, I liken it to this example: imagine you are in a village, surrounded by all you've ever known and dreamed of, and are reasonably content, except you have an 'intuitive' nagging doubt that there is more to life and an instinct to leave. This will be the soul calling!

However, each time you begin the journey out of the village, all you can see around you is barren land, mountain ranges and nothing of interest, no apparent life, no real light. So taking the journey is not only unpleasant, but it also seems futile.

So you don't go, or each time you start out, you tell yourself all the reasons that it makes no sense to continue and you turn around and head back.

The only thing is, what you can't see – but your soul intelligence can – is that across the other side of that mountain range is another much bigger village full of wondrous adventure and fulfilment for you!

I also hasten to add that sometimes our resistance isn't always more obviously about *coming out* of a situation, it can also be about going *into* a situation – such as a relationship. Either way what's happening is you are resisting change. We can throw up as many justifications as we like about not wanting change, but we have to work out what we are resisting and access our soul consciousness, work out what it wants and take the walk into the unknown!

We also sometimes refer to this part of our journey as 'a

dark night of the soul' experience. All you have is faith and that sense of inner knowing of the soul, and if you trust it you'll end up somewhere much better.

And what happened for me, upon deciding to leave my father's house completely encapsulates what I'm trying to communicate here. So I more or less decided I needed to go...but where? My conscious mind and value judgements kicked in with all the sensible options of what to do next: I researched renting, or sharing new places, moving cities, and also had the possibility of living at a local Buddhist centre. My conscious mind at the time put that option way down the list of possibilities, favouring a house share elsewhere.

So what did I do? I went and danced! I danced at a local 5Rhythms class (it's a kind of spontaneous free-form dance practice, non-choreographed so you don't have to 'think', which thus has the ability to help you bypass your 'left' brain which comes up with intelligent answers and access your right brain, which is connected to a much broader level of awareness, i.e. your soul), and bang, in a flash I found myself having a vision of moving into the Buddhist centre. So I did, and it was good!

And this is how I do my internal navigation – it's not always dance or visions – sometimes I get a feeling or what seems like a gentle whisper while in the deep relaxation at the end of a yoga class, walking in nature, or while meditating or sometimes running.

And sometimes I just feel clear enough no matter what I'm doing, and this is the point we are trying to move towards, that we become clear enough and familiar enough with it to recognise the whisper of the soul throughout our daily lives!

I feel my soul does, in some aspects of my life, also have a sense of destination, although to some degree I also have to fill in the gaps as I go along. That's where the fun is and paying attention to what opportunities the universe presents to you: look out for the buzz in your heart as it will tell you when something is relevant. For me, it's all about healing work – in all areas of my life, but also spreading the word of body-mind wisdom far and wide.

So while that stays as a broader sense of destination, every now and again I can see shorter term projects that emerge moving towards that. At times it's been intensively offering acupuncture, or teaching yoga, offering retreats, and the latest vision is with this book, writing articles and public speaking, but I know it will continue to evolve as the soul is a consumer of experiences! As soon as it becomes familiar with something and you've walked through one creative doorway, you can be sure another will appear!

And remember, it's also not always about the big stuff and overall life direction; your soul prompts you about everything: relationships, getting up and doing exercises, making the phone call to your loved ones you've been putting off, and putting away the serious stuff and over-application by going out and having fun. Or vice versa!

Nuts and Bolts: Tutorial

The soul terminology

I'm aware that using terminology which refers to less tangible phenomena such as the soul (some people also think of it as a 'higher self') can be evocative and challenging for some who have a more scientific and rational background. Or, even if you accept it on a deep subconscious level, often the conscious rational mind has a hard time accepting it anyway!

However, for the purposes of being coached by me, it's not actually important that you subscribe fully to the idea you have a soul with all the bells and whistles that may come attached to that with notions of previous lives and so on. I don't go into that. All that is important is that you are conscious you have an element of individuality that is unique to you. It doesn't really matter whether you think it's a result of having a soul with a unique set of characteristics, or just a result of your experiences in this life, you just have to subscribe to the idea that you are unique and there is part of you where that information is contained.

For the sceptics out there, I want you to look at how the concepts of heart and soul often crop up in our everyday language when we've had a really raw human experience – one that bypasses our more superficial intellect. Even the most hardened of scientific minds might occasionally let slip the phrase 'I put my heart and soul into that' or that there is some 'soul searching' to do or how something can be 'soul destroying' when something we've worked for that is meaningful goes awry. When we've had a very raw, almost mortal experience people do often talk of being touched to the very soul of their being. Just something to think about!

What am I?

You are a combination of your unique soul, which sits within your body and your more physical level disposition, tendencies and personality that come from your genetic lineage, i.e. your ancestral line.

Your soul can be seen as an aspect of you that is constantly witnessing the decisions and actions that you take in life, often delivering promptings for change. I like to think of the soul as the part of me that is the deepest part of me watching what I'm doing from behind my eyes.

The blueprint and prompting for creative evolution

All of creation has a natural blueprint that enables it to thrive and find its maximum potential; it's just in-built. Have a look around: nature, the planet, animals and plant life, it all just does by instinct what it needs to do. The planet and universe have been here for billions of years, and just creatively evolve, so it stands a chance that within its very fabric is an intelligence that guides it to do so.

This is notwithstanding that we often interfere with and damage the natural processes of life around us from doing what they do to stay balanced. Indeed, we often sabotage the natural life around us from doing what it needs to do, just like we often sabotage our own personal evolution, or that of others, due to a disconnection with our own instincts and over-reliance on errant intelligence and misguided beliefs.

However, what differentiates us as human beings from the natural life around us, in some respects, is that we have a different level of consciousness and ability for acute self-awareness. So, whereas an animal or plant may by instinct or design do what it needs to thrive, it may not have the same level of self-awareness of those actions or instincts as you have.

KEY POINT

I am establishing two things here: firstly, just like the rest of the universe, you have a blueprint for balance and creative evolution guiding and passing through you to help you thrive. And secondly, with the additional human capacity for self-awareness, you also have the ability to access and be aware of the blueprint!

So where is and what is the blueprint? It's your soul.

Your soul is your blueprint and your instincts are how you feel and express it, and flow with its guidance to keep you creatively evolving just like life around you. The whole experience of accessing your soul comes with a couple of different 'flavours' – you get an individual essence of what you need to do, but also an awareness of the universal rules you need to play by (such as yin and yang and the Five Elements, which I will detail in later chapters) in order to maintain balance on the way.

So we need regular means of accessing the intelligence of and listening to the soul which is an ongoing process, and where the natural healing arts and activities can be of great use which I will also discuss later.

For people who don't often access the intelligence of the soul, when they do, they can often put it down to an unusual experience and often seek to quickly drown that voice back out – particularly if life isn't going so well. This is because the promptings of the soul can be very creatively challenging if we aren't really on track with our highest potential, striking like a dagger at who we 'think' we are, and the various constructs we have about our identity. So if we are way off our 'blueprint' then the whisper of the soul can be tricky to listen to, as it can throw a curveball at who we think we are and what we think we are meant to be doing! However ultimately, it's the voice you need to learn to trust.

We often experience these moments of accessing the soul as moments of 'insight'. A moment of insight is where you are witnessing your life from your soul level, accessing soul consciousness, and it's communicating through to your personality level mind. The personality level mind is often shaped through experiences as we evolve, the tendencies, opinions of those around us, and our genetic nuances. It gives you personality, but the various themes and voices you hear in your mind might not actually 'belong' to you as such. It can be likened to the tip of the iceberg, but what's in the depths – in the subconscious – can be of a vastly different shape.

The voice of the soul often sits further into this subconscious, which is why we need practices that enable us to quieten the mind so we can dip into those deeper soulful levels of who we are. Then the essences and voice of the soul can start to make its way from the subconscious to inform the personality level mind – so you might still have your unique quirks and nuances, but the underlying driver to your actions, opinions and thoughts starts to come more from the intelligence of the soul, rather than collective norms and opinions of others.

Self-witnessing requires you to view yourself from a different vantage point – if you don't think you have a soul or higher self, who exactly do you think is doing the witnessing in these moments of insight or self-realisation?

For more on soul, personality and insight
please visit this blog: Soul & Personality[ii]

---

ii   www.creativewellness.co.uk/bookblogs

You can also sometimes think of moments when you access the soul as 'peak experiences' and sometimes you may not have chosen to heed the wisdom of these. Maybe you have done a workshop or had a particularly soulful moment (a moment of 'clarity'), but then returned back to your highly patterned life and fell back to 'sleep' again, nostalgically reminiscing about the experience you had. Try living your entire life on the peak!

Life is an ongoing creative process

Well here's the news, life doesn't start and stop like that! It's an ongoing creative process and we need to keep accessing the intelligence of it regularly. In some respects even talking about the soul as if it's a different entity to who we are is also actually a slight misnomer. It's part of who we are, only we can tend to identify more strongly with other streams of dialogue we hear in our mind, like our intellect, personality tendencies, self-opinions or opinions we have picked up from others. So the soul can seem like a distant part of us, a different voice.

People also often talk about hearing the voice of the soul as a kind of 'intuition' – but again referencing it as if that voice comes from somewhere external to us and doesn't actually belong or originate within us, which shows a misunderstanding of what intuition is.

Intuition = Inner tuition

That voice or prompting/gut feeling comes from within you. Intuition = inner tuition. Similarly, people may also think of it in the context of a 'gut feeling'. And indeed, the reason that 'gut feeling' is an appropriate metaphor is that Chinese medicine actually identifies that the gut and the heart are 'energetically' connected[3]. When you are an embryo they are actually fused together and maintain a communication link throughout your life so what your heart is feeling is often reflected in the sensation within your gut.

This misconception around the origin of 'intuition' is similar to how people often misinterpret the concept of destiny, which is another concept we can closely associate to that of soul. Once again, destiny isn't a set of circumstances that happens to us from the outside (or even if you think it is there isn't anything you can do about it anyway). In the context of this work, destiny is the reference to your internal soul blueprint so destiny is actually a reflection and expression of what's within you.

Being close to your destiny simply means being close to and expressing the deepest layers of your authentic being – individual to you. You can also swap it around with the term 'life purpose' if that feels more comfortable.

For more on destiny please visit this blog: Destiny[iii]

When we have taken advice from someone, they often, but not always, are basing it on their own experiences or value judgements on external factors and cannot fully appreciate the fullness of your own position, so being able to find answers within is very valuable. Please note, I'm not dismissing seeking help, as sometimes people can act as a mirror to find our own answers or therapeutically assist us in getting balanced to find our truth and inner voice.

---

iii   www.creativewellness.co.uk/bookblogs

Being present and having presence - the heart electromagnetic field

Accessing the soul has a particularly high vibration (high energy!) to it so it makes you feel incredibly well and you tend to have a sense of presence – people pay you more attention. Soulful moments also tend to be characterised by feeling very 'present' within the experience with little other internal dialogue/chatter inhabiting the mind. This is also explained in various therapeutic modalities as being a result of the increase of the electromagnetic field of the heart that occurs in these moments.

It's this increase in your electromagnetic field or 'aura' which makes you more noticeable to others and also relaxes and quiets discordance in other organs and aspects of the nervous system that otherwise creates additional thoughts. The organs and nervous system are impacted as they are also essentially bathed within your heart energy – it's also why people around you might also feel more relaxed in your company, but in fact not just the people, but the plants and animals around you too. You feed the whole.

Put quite simply, when you are doing soulful activities, your heart and body-mind are happy and there is no need to overthink or be overstimulated (stressed)!

Doing a large amount of soulful activities also leaves a positive legacy in your actual physical body. We identified above that when you are doing a soulful activity your heart radiance increases, and since your heart processes blood, it stamps onto the fluids of the body the essence of your soul which becomes part of your physical vibration and body-mind here and now. You start to radiate a soulful and authentic presence. However, this needs renewal – the more soulful activities we do, the more presence we have as the soulful charge stays within the body.

This would reflect in what we think of as someone having a great deal of charisma, a good 'vibe' or presence. When someone is truly doing what they love, their energy field 'aura' extends massively off the body. Think of a performer truly in their essence or when you walk into a room where someone has been creatively inspired or in their 'element'. You can often feel their presence in the atmosphere. So when you do what you love, you become a radiant and inspiring person with a sense of presence.

You can also contrast and consider your own internal experience of when you don't really want to be doing something. Think of how we even say in our everyday language, "My heart wasn't really in it" when we feel we have moved on from something or it just doesn't work well for us. You could actually swap 'heart' for 'soul' in this instance since, as we have identified, there is an intimate connection between the two.

Getting to know your heart

Getting to know the energetic qualities and characteristics of the heart is an essential ally in your ability to relate to the promptings and expression of the soul. I have already made reference to the relationship between the heart and soul, that the soul uses the heart as a navigation and expression tool (as the essence of the soul sits in the heart). Therefore it makes sense that if we understand some of the basic characteristics and feelings of the heart in expression and reception then we can more clearly interpret the promptings of the soul.

When we *feel* something in the heart it has particular importance. This is because energetically the heart sits midway – as the middle chakra (see Chapter 3) – between our grounded physical reality and the etheric[4], collective consciousness and soul source above us.

Put in simple terms, we can sometimes be going about our Earthly day-to-day business without it being particularly meaningful to us, or sometimes we can be drifting around in our dreams and visions in our mind, which can come from the soul speaking to us.

However, the heart is where these two forces of grounded reality and soul intelligence meet, so when you feel something in your heart it has meaning, right now in this moment. It's the junction of your soul and physical reality.

Key indicators of these 'heart opening' moments are an actual opening sensation in the chest, a straightening of the spine, a sensation of lightness and wellbeing, and what can feel like a cool chill passing through your being – 'goosebumps'. If you are speaking with someone and something particularly authentic or light is spoken both of you may feel this uplift!

For more on heart energy please visit this blog:
The Electromagnetic Field of The Heart[iv]

The soul is often the quietest voice

We can often become disconnected from the voice of our soul if we don't regularly have the means to engage with it, or express our soulful nature, and it can also create a situation

---

iv   www.creativewellness.co.uk/bookblogs

where other voices in our mind become particularly loud as there is lack of direction from and ability to hear the messages of the soul.

In fact, if we have been particularly disconnected from the voice and energy of the soul, we can really become quite closed to it, and old imprints, habit patterns and fears can almost totally overrun our mind to the point that we question whether those more soulful experiences and feelings we'd previously had could even be real or true. These other voices like to keep us safe and familiar – hence the dreaded comfort zone – but it's best not to indulge them and focus more on heartfelt and soulful activities which lift us and continually pull us out of 'falling asleep'.

In Chinese medicine, we actually refer to the heart as the quietest voice you hear in your mind, so when the mind is busy it's competing with some pretty loud competition! This is also why it's essential to get to know the various streams of dialogue you hear in your mind (which I cover in Chapter 5) so you can have some discernment. It's also important to clear up your energetic body[5] (see 'Therapeutic subtleties – the impact of discordant energy' in Chapter 7) and quiet the discordant chatter with therapies and by cultivating practices in your routine that help this, such as yoga, meditation and deep relaxation. The mind gets busier when we are off track in life as the other organs, elements and aspects of our nervous system are trying to dictate our next move to create balance, basically trying to take over the role of the soul as we can't connect with it. At this stage it's as though you are walking in the dark, taking haphazard guesses at things that you think might help!

It's worth noting this important point. Even when you've

come back to balance and cleared up your energetic body, and the discordant chatter has quietened and you are feeling happy and well, it's not always the case of having an 'empty' mind. Sitting in deep meditation, we can still sometimes hear the voice of the heart and soul as a distinct voice within, only it's a much more distinct and comfortable voice, as the other discordant voices are quiet. The voice of the soul can also be felt, and experienced, as a direct subtle energetic transmission of light, which can also be accessed and realised through deep meditation, but in many cases it can be distinctly interpreted through words or visions.

In Chapter 5, I will explore in greater detail where the other voices we hear in our mind come from, and their relationship to heart and soul, as it's very important in developing our understanding of our 'internal' world. What's important at this stage is understanding that when we are in alignment, the soul sits in the heart with such efficacy and power that it directs the other organs and elements within us.

The greater intelligence of soul consciousness and true wisdom of listening to your heart

The soul essence within you is also plugged into a much broader consciousness and intelligence than the narrower personality mind we can often inhabit which relies a lot on logic and creating new preconceptions and expectations based on old experiences. This is because your soul essence (or soul seed) is connected to the soul source where a great deal of the overall choreography of your life is orchestrated and guided from.

Thus, since the heart is the tool of expression of the soul

and where we experience soul intelligence in the body, then truly following your heart is actually the ultimate level of intelligence and way to navigate through life. The old saying of listening to your heart isn't an empty cliché, as although it may not always make sense to the more logical mind, remember it is connected to a much broader perspective than you can see from your own vantage point, and in time events unfold which may make more sense. Think of it as your soul having access to the soul source that has an entire 360-degree perspective on all life and can be busy making connections for you that you can't see – yet! So, trust the impulse of the heart.

It's like the difference between being lost in a crowd trying to find your way out as opposed to being able to see the entire crowd from above and plotting a route based on the bigger picture.

Passion is a barometer for how much your
soul is engaged in what you are doing!

The human energetic anatomy when in alignment

In balance, the heart is the supreme controller and commander of the other organs in the body, which can be divided into yin and yang organs (depending on whether they are more focused on storage and conservation – yin, or transformation and transportation – yang) and are also categorised into elements which all play a role in aspects of our human experience. These elements express in a number of ways including behaviours, emotions and thoughts.

Therefore the job of the various elements within us

is to listen to the promptings of the soul, and, working in relationship with the natural forces that govern life on the planet, to create the conditions for us to thrive. This is what we experience as our instincts as nature is designed to balance us – it's built into everything.

So what can get in the way and go wrong in our balance process?

Confusion

> You can think of confusion as meaning 'consciousness fusion'. Basically, you end up getting lots of voices fused together in your mind and don't know which is most efficacious to follow!

When we don't do enough activities or practices that align us to our soul then the various elements within us get confused and misaligned – they start to try and take over the running of our life which can create imbalances.

Imbalances in the various elements

The voice of the heart and soul can speak to the various elements, but when they are imbalanced they can get into a kind of energetic paralysis or stilted expression. The message might come through to the organs which make up the elements, but if they are injured they can't respond to the call. Five Element acupuncture can be a great system to help this (as it works directly with elements and organs) as can of course yoga, meditation and other therapies. Just 'being' and doing things you love with your soul thoroughly in your body is also incredibly healing.

Old imprints/memories which get in the way of accurate decision making

Just in the same way that the voice of the heart and soul can imprint on the blood and fluids of the body when we do things that we love (since the blood gets pumped by the heart, it becomes infused with the vibration of the heart) so similarly things that we don't like – situations, feelings, emotions, things people have said to us – can also begin to imprint on the body and afflict us negatively.

We explore in Chapter 3 and 7 in greater detail the mechanics of how vibration affects our body-mind. However, so you can garner some appreciation of how significant this can be, just imagine for a moment standing in front of a large stack of speakers blasting loud music and how you can literally feel the vibration hitting your body. And importantly reflect on how the sound of the music can stay bouncing around in you afterwards, and for how long you can often hear the sounds in your mind. In a similar way you can imagine how the vibration of other experiences can also stay and bounce around in you – literally permeating the fluids and air in the body.

Interestingly Dr Masaru Emoto tries to illustrate in even greater detail the process of how fluids are impacted by what they are exposed to. In his book *Hidden Messages in Water*[6] he documents his findings of how water crystals are affected by different thoughts and feelings. Although there is some debate about his findings – as there often is with subtle phenomena as it's difficult to measure – this would give some indication as to the degree of subtlety in the way the vibration of things around us can impact.

Similarly to how fluids are impacted, you can also reflect

on how air becomes tainted by what it's exposed to – reflect on the sense of 'atmosphere' that resides in a place sometimes long after an activity has ceased.

So, since the body contains so much fluid and air, the experiences we engage with can create imprints upon them which can in turn become embedded as memories and patterns and part of our mental landscape. Traumatic or unpleasant experiences can create negative inner chatter about ourselves and limiting judgements and beliefs designed to try and keep us 'safe' in future.

In a sense, what we engage with becomes part of who we are and we need to watch out for these discordant voices (neatly referred to as 'trolls' by embodiment coach Mark Walsh[7]). Something to look out for is that they tend to have a repetitive voice – every situation in life is actually unique with a unique set of possibilities, so if your mind is playing out the same old inner chatter and opinions then chances are it's one of your old 'trolls'.

These 'trolls' can come from things that we are told when we are younger, but can then later become things that we start to tell ourselves, so we actually even lose awareness of their origin. Or they can come from opinions that we form of ourselves when we are younger which are often due to a limited set of circumstances, i.e. the family unit or school life.

When this happens and the repetitive voice of things you have been told or experienced in the past gets in the way of you moving forward this is essentially 'conditioning' getting in the way of your soul promptings.

Due to these inputs being such significant formative and lengthy experiences, they can lend themselves to us forming opinions of our self which are totally subjective to that situation and inaccurate to the broader whole of who we are and other capacities we have. Other qualities that we have at that point may well be unseen – as we haven't had the people around us at that point to draw them out so we don't know how great we can be!

For example, when I was younger, within my family unit I was considered shy, but looking back that really was relative to the dynamic of my family, not an 'absolute'. Adopting that behaviour fitted well to keep the balance to some degree within my family, and taking that label on meant I could hide a bit socially too. In some ways it was also a way of getting sympathy and, actually, thus attention in some respects!

Similarly, at school, I was considered a bit sensitive but I felt it came tagged, by others, with a slightly negative undertone, almost as if it was a fault to be sensitive! This perception in part was again due to the relativity of the people around me, who perhaps couldn't understand the way I experienced life, but these kinds of opinions can just stick, for the people around you and in your own mind!

For the record, I don't actually think I'm shy at all. It took me about 30 years to work that one out; being around people who I really resonate with taught me that. Anyone who's met, lived or worked with me over the last few years will testify I've generally got plenty to say and plenty of confidence – particularly now I'm full of soul as I'm doing the things I love more! And my sensitivity is most definitely a strength in the line of occupation I do; it just wasn't particularly noticed as such within the slightly harsher backdrop of my school life.

So these discordant voices or 'trolls' tend to be repetitive, and when we let our vibration drop, i.e. stop accessing soul consciousness, these voices can start to kick back in with a vengeance which is why it's important to know what they are and keep in your mind the creative voice of the soul from when you have accessed it, i.e. keep the faith! And also don't forget that we integrate positive energy into the body-mind in the same way as we integrate discordant energy, so engaging with sources of high vibration energy to help re-inspire and reshape your perception is always a good idea!

Habit patterns

Additionally, our own memories of what we have already done previously in this life can also start to influence our actions as they can create a strong imprint.

As human beings, we have a tendency to create habit patterns. Just notice when you have a new, satisfying or memorable experience, such as the first time you visit a city and find a particularly good restaurant, how it can very quickly become a pattern to want to revisit this same place, even order the same food. We play out these patterns across a very broad spectrum of our behaviour – from the most basic of eating, sleeping and exercising, through to more elaborate patterns.

When we get stuck in patterns it can often be like we are sleepwalking in routines, the patterns become so thickly layered that we continually just play them out. Eat, sleep, work, repeat. What we did yesterday or last week becomes what we are doing again today. Again, remember that each situation in life is actually unique so if you are repeating the same stuff over, then check you aren't trapped in your comfort zone!

At the end of the day, the way out of these particular scenarios isn't to fight with or reason with the voices in your mind but just to keep accessing the greater intelligence of soul consciousness which raises your vibration and radiance to fulfil your being with spontaneity. As explained earlier, this also reduces the volume of the other discordant chatter in the mind (trolls) as well as being much more alluring and efficacious, and will over time begin to change the imprints on the body too.

So, while acupuncture and treatments can also work to alleviate significantly embedded and discordant energies that sit within the body, you still need to work at refilling yourself afterwards with the good soulful stuff!

It's also good to notice that since it feels so fulfilling when you have really been soul embodied, there is also a tendency to reach out much less to other things to pick your energy up, whether it's food, drink or seeking attention from other people (as opposed to connecting with other people simply as a gift of life). You just feel more nourished and less needy!

In some form or another, around any area of your life there are always multiple perspectives, often that contradict each other about what you should be doing. So, all you can do, at the centre of that, is trust what feels right. It's the only common factor, what's in your own special heart.

Soul and personality

I opened the chapter by explaining how we are a combination of our soul and genetic, ancestral tendencies which also create our expression and demeanour in life.

And while the promptings of our soul are always what we are looking for, it's also helpful to be aware that over time, what happens is that the radiance of your soul, the more you engage with it, starts to take over from your genetic, predisposed version of self that you are born with.

Essentially, your soul consciousness starts to permeate your conscious expression, and you start to become a generally more 'soulful' person, enabling you to drop old tendencies which you might have picked up habitually or been influenced by in your early life, but that aren't your authentic self.

This embodiment of soul is a continual process, and like much else we discuss, can also have a yin and yang quality to it, in the sense that after a concerted period of soul growth, we may have relatively fallow periods where we integrate our experiences to become part of our body-mind and shape our future spontaneous expression in the world.

But there's no rush – you just follow your instincts and freewheel when you need to while you integrate new possibilities and experiences, and then when the impetus comes to pedal like fury and be the change in your life, expressing this more refined version of yourself in the world, then do that too! Life carries you through this process.

Ways to listen to and embody the soul

In summary, practices which embody the soul can be individual to you as it evidently depends on your own unique nature and what 'switches you on'. However, by quieting the mind, we can begin to hear our soul voice much more clearly, and then get on with creating the circumstances that it desires for growth and embodied presence (a sense that the qualities and desires of the soul are really being lived out and fulfilled in your life now). While embodiment activities are very individual, there tend to be a few more common activities and themes that enable us to hear the voice of the soul within.

Time spent in nature – walking in particular

Urban backdrops are very discordant to our subtle awareness as they are so chaotic, noisy and over stimulating. When we move in a much less discordant environment such as nature it harmonises our nervous system and we can often 'hear' our deeper self much more clearly. Using nature to access the voice of the soul is deeply rooted in our ancestry. At the more intensive end of the spectrum you have the soul searching 'vision quests', often associated with indigenous cultures (who are generally more attuned to natural wisdom) which would consist of extended periods of time in nature. Spending this time in nature takes away irritating electromagnetic energy that is prevalent in urban settings and interferes with our subtle perception by irritating our third eye chakra (a nerve plexus in the forehead that is associated with perception and intuition).

The silence during yoga, meditation or deep relaxation

Similarly to what happens when you spend time in nature, these practices calm the nervous system and allow you to hear the deeper intelligence in you. This is also the ultimate intention, when I teach these practices, to facilitate others to find this place inside themselves. We will dedicate an entire section of this book to the benefits of yoga, mindfulness, meditation and deep relaxation later. Freestyle (non-choreographed) dance such as 5Rhythms or Movement Medicine can also have a similar effect.

Over time you may of course notice other activities that enable you to hear this deep and precious part of yourself.

Ways to notice that your soul is more embodied

Feeling present and confident

The expression of the soul tends to be spontaneous and fluidly animated as you do not have to 'think' about what to do; you are just expressing a deep level of authentic self.

Good posture

Since the soul exudes through the heart, you'll often find that your chest opens and spine extends when your soul is embodied.

Less internal chatter

As previously explained, when the soul is embodied in the heart then other organs feel soothed and create much less internal chatter (which is related to their energetic state).

Repetitive patterns (comfort zone) and addictive patterns tend to fall away

When you are connected to your soul, you become more spontaneous so repetitive patterns – that are to your detriment – tend to fall away. And when you are doing what you love it provides a subtle sense of nourishment and energetically raises your vibration and soothes the internal agitation which comes from organs when they are stressed. This allays the addictive tendencies we have when the organs are distressed.

Exercises: The soul

1. What activities or situations do you do where you feel able to access a deep part of yourself and really 'hear yourself think' e.g. long walks, meditations, etc?
2. What activities or situations do you do in your life that make you feel your soul is embodied?

These points might help:

There are often themes which emerge as to when our soul feels switched on – I call it 'looking for the clues'. You can make a list of types of situations when you feel soul embodied, and look for common themes – perhaps there's an activity in common?

My example: My soul feels switched on when I'm doing virtually anything to do with holistic health – treating, teaching, etc.

Make some observations of your posture in particular situations. Look for the connection to your gut instinct as well via the heart – when you feel comfortable in your belly you are often 'embodied'. When your gut/abdomen freezes your heart is also often closed.

3. Reflect on times when you have been stuck in a rut, heavily in patterns of thought and habitual actions, and then done something you have enjoyed. Reflect on how it changed your mindset and feelings and perhaps even pulled you out of those habitual patterns for a while. Make a note of three occasions and also how long that uplifting effect lasted for.

If you are struggling:

a) Think, what did you do as a child? If you are struggling to identify what you naturally move towards doing through simple, innate passion, then it can be useful to think back to what activities you were naturally drawn to as a child. Without the pressures of adult life, and the imposition of what we 'think' we should be doing, we would often just gravitate to activities that we loved doing. These activities can evidently evolve as we get older (although the essence of the activity can remain the same) but in this instance, it's as much about trying to reflect on how you felt while doing those activities – at one, happy and content. It's time to find the same feelings in your life and activities now.

b) Imagine you were stranded on a desert island with 30 other people, what would you do? What role would you naturally be drawn to? Would you want to be the cook? Would you want to help build? Dig holes? Collect food? Would you want to plan and organise the structure of how to get things done? Would you be the healer? The entertainer? The gardener? The organiser of the living space? What area would you naturally like to take charge of?

3

Understanding Interconnectedness

My journey into connection

I used to see the world as full of separate objects, with boundaries created by their *physical* structure. Thus, unless something physically touched something else, then I believed it had no real significant relationship or connection with what was around it.

Even when considering humans, unless there was actual contact, I would also see separate beings. It appeared that people acted solely under their own intelligence with their choices in life, each person creating their own sense of direction from within and acting upon it.

I suspect this way of seeing the world full of separate beings and entities is relatively prevalent in the Western culture and the idea that there could be some kind of interconnecting force, or greater intelligence dictating or choreographing the movement of people, plants, animals and natural life generally, well, that wouldn't even have crossed my conscious mind!

However, there were some glaring exceptions where a sense of non-physical interconnection between people or objects was particularly apparent, which gave me the awareness that there was some influence that people or objects could have on each other without physical touch. And this kind of awareness was really my first stepping stone into understanding so much more!

Firstly, it is never lost on me how at a football match, or motorbike speedway meeting, with thousands of other people, there is an acknowledgement that those people in attendance can create an 'atmosphere' – something which hangs in the air radiating from these people, something which is created beyond their physical interaction, but yet which collectively influences everybody present.

Sure, some of these people might be physically touching or brushing against each other occasionally, particularly when you used to be able to stand at football grounds, but even so there was an acknowledgement that something else, more subtle, but still powerful, can be created by the presence of these people. A subtle radiance that could alter the way people think and feel.

Secondly, I would probably, like most of us, be conscious of how the presence of just one other person near me could affect how I felt. Just one other person, standing in front of me, without touch, could make me feel vastly different, evoke vastly different emotions in me, depending on who they were. Standing next to someone at a bus stop could make me open into conversation or contract and shy away – by sheer instinct.

Thirdly, I remember being aware of this sense of interconnection and atmosphere on a more global level too. I'll never forget the second 'Live Aid' or Live 8 event held in 2005.

From the time I woke up that morning, I could tangibly feel the whole 'atmosphere' of my street and town was different, and felt the same as I visited the neighbouring city too! The positive activities and intentions of so many people seemingly influenced more than the immediate space around them, with the impact on a national and perhaps global level that day.

And of course, we have even more subtle, almost quaint examples of our interconnection with others, like when we are thinking of someone and they 'coincidentally' just happen to call us on the phone at that same moment. I've actually personally had numerous times where I've pulled my phone out of my pocket (even if it's on silent) when someone is calling so I've not just been experiencing the awareness of connection on a thought level, but it can also seemingly influence my spontaneous actions too!

Another common occurrence I notice related to my work is that if I've been working abroad for a while and schedule a trip back to England – or start the journey back – then I'll get an influx of emails regarding receiving acupuncture with me, or enquiring about me teaching a workshop. And a favourite synchronicity is that often, when I take some time to sort through old patients' notes and update my filing, I will have people I haven't treated in months or years suddenly contacting me, seemingly responding to the fact I was thinking of them!

But, like a great number of other subtle 'unseen' life dynamics, it's often just generally a bit too confronting and difficult for the mind to try to concretely define and give credibility to these 'unseen' dynamics. And who was I meant to ask anyway? Back when I was growing up there was no internet and such existential and ethereal subjects weren't exactly the topics of choice with the people around me!

However, nonetheless, these things I was becoming aware of were beginning to inform and develop my understanding of interconnection, and prompting me to try and define some of the mechanics and patterns involved.

Taking all the above examples, it was relatively easy for me to start building a case that there must be unseen channels of communication directly between people, as people are the common denominator in all cases – they all involve people 'radiating' something and other people picking it up in their awareness.

However, the question would then deepen: just how far does this ability of 'unseen' and less 'tangible' forces extend in its capacity to influence our mind and human life? Can those subtle signals be from the inherent balancing intelligence of the universe itself 'talking' to you, rather than just another person?

Because, as I'll discuss further shortly, nature is designed to keep its own balance; it has an intelligence behind it, so since you are also part of nature – even though we forget this – it makes sense it will also act on you just like it acts on other forms of life.

And because we also have the capacity for self-awareness of what passes through our mind and therefore the capacity to access the 'creative blueprint' – as I discussed in the previous chapter – perhaps some of the signals we actually hear in our minds are nature and insight into a 'universal intelligence' guiding us.

So my inquiry expanded to also become about unravelling and understanding the various levels of interconnection, and how we might distinguish or experience them in the body and mind.

Let's have a deeper look at the example of where we think of someone just as they call us on the phone, as it could appear there might be several different possibilities of interconnection going on there!

On first appraisal, we could just think that the other person has thought of us, and it's popped into our mind and we are aware of it.

Or perhaps we could consider that we might be giving off a conscious or subconscious thought about them, that they are responding to in calling us. So the question is, who actually starts the chain reaction?

Or, and this is where it gets really interesting, perhaps neither person is actually the 'originator' as such, but instead this impulse to connect is actually created for us, by the intelligence of the universe and nature itself, and that is what we are responding to. Part of nature's way of keeping balance in that particular moment is to connect you together.

Just in the same way that meeting someone on the physical plane brings a particular essence to your energy field, so when we think of someone it connects a subtle vibrational essence to you on a more etheric plane. And the appearance in each other's mind is simply occurring due to your ability to have insight and self-awareness into that impulse for you to connect.

But how do we even know the universe has some kind of intelligence to it, of how it connects things together to bring balance? Well just look around – the planet has been around for over four billion years, and there does appear to be some rhyme and reason to how it organises natural life, which we'll also explore on one level in the following chapter on natural forces.

The key, as I will discuss later, is in understanding that you are also part of natural life, so you are also part of the interconnected web of consciousness and vast ecosystem that acts as a consolidated force to maintain balance. Basically, it's about trusting that the universe does know what it's doing and that it will move you accordingly, in relationship to what's going on around you to keep you in balance. It will move you physically, mentally, emotionally and spiritually. So to deny this impulse is just you getting in the way of nature's calling to keep you balanced!

> We live in a great universal 'One'. Within that 'One' in any given moment you have a place, where in balance your energy meets the world to enable you to be fully whole, to feel at 'One'. It's a path of exploration, where our energy will constantly moment to moment lead us and be drawn toward those energies and vibrations which lead to balance and health.

> In any one moment this may be being the party king or queen, sitting quietly in a park, planning your day tomorrow or reflecting on yesterday; following this natural flow we maintain balance and health and forcing against this flow or being inhibited from it results in dis-ease.
> **Richard Brook, 2004**

> We heal each moment because this is what universal energy seeks to do.
> **Richard Brook, 2004**

Just as a bee gets attracted to a flower to draw its pollen and then flies off to make honey, while pollinating extra life on the way, perhaps our instinctive actions, thoughts and inclinations are just simply also a part of a vaster system of balance.

For example, thinking of a loved one and their acts of kindness after an unpleasant encounter with someone else can be just nature's way of keeping balance. Just like after a period of heat, nature can bring the rain to keep balance.

My journey was – and still is – trying to recognise some of these dynamics. Which thoughts and impulses am I having that feel creative and evolutionary and are drawing me into connection with balancing forces – other people, places, events that are beneficial – and which thoughts are more like junk mail?

Because while I'm sure some of the thoughts I'm conscious of in my mind are actually from the intelligence of the universe, I'm also sure that some of what pops into my mental inbox sometimes is actually 'junk mail' rather than being from the 'head of creative', so to speak!

How do I know the difference? Well the junk mail tends to be memories, and feel heavy, whereas the intelligent stuff that is the universe driving me into beneficial connections, well that feels lighter, present and more creative. Because what does nature ever create that is exactly the same as something else? Nothing, not that I know of anyway! Dolly the cloned sheep wasn't quite nature's own original doing, was she!

So nature is constantly, due to being in a state of perpetual change, creating new possibilities for you to grow and move which you see in your self-awareness, your 'insight mechanism'. But then another level of your mind can often get in the way, which is why a massive part of this work is about getting rid of old stagnant energy in the body and mind, which creates the 'junk mail' and repetitive patterns in your mind, and is also about engaging in practices which get you beyond the smaller, narrower mind into the more creative, spontaneous aspect of who you are – and what you can be!

5Rhythms Dance really helped to increase my awareness of this broader level of interconnection considerably. Not only does it enable you to transcend the narrower aspect of your mind into the more expansive, creative mind (dance and free movement facilitates this; see Chapter 7) but I would observe how someone would move to a particular position on the dance floor and others then move in relation – not because it was choreographed, but because it was instinct. This is life; everyone and everything is always moving in relationship.

But also think about how this happens on other levels. When you are around someone radiating a particular emotion, it can move your own emotions in relation; on the mental level, when someone is articulating their thoughts, it has the capacity to move and change your own thoughts, and spiritually, when someone radiates a subtle 'spiritual' essence, it has the capacity to move your own sense of spirit too – to uplift and give a renewed sense of life purpose.

But what is the mechanics of how this process of influence works? It's vibration and resonance. Vibration and resonance is the medium of how people feel the influence of not only others around them, even without physical touch, but also everything else in their sphere of awareness, since everything in existence vibrates on some level.

So, the same way that the person standing in front of me radiated a vibration that affected me, so does a dog, a cat, a tree, a plant, the food in front of me, the concrete or earth underneath me and even the air around me, and indeed what may be in the air – aromas, pollutants, other planets in the solar system. As they move about closer and further from the Earth they have an impact too!

And of course, as I mentioned earlier, someone thinking of me, even if they are many miles away, that also has a subtle vibration which can trigger resonance in me (the science aspect of which can also be explained in quantum mechanics, should you prefer that approach).

So, from the smallest to the largest, the fact is that all matter vibrates to some degree – so it all radiates and affects what's around it. When I started to understand this, then it started to make sense to me why being around certain people affected me the way it did.

And also, I started to understand that it doesn't matter what I 'think' of these people, whatever 'spin' I want to put on it on a mental, interpretative level, it doesn't matter as there is a tangible vibration that these people give off that hits my nervous system and has an impact.

Yes, I'll say that again, sometimes no matter what mental level spin you wish to put on something, the object still has a tangible vibration that hits you, which can be stimulating or exciting, neutral, or sometimes abrasive or creating friction.

To go even deeper we can also identify that when a vibration hits your own energy field, hits your own vibration, the two vibrations interact together to either create something else – sometimes like nice music (that you and everyone and everything else present can bathe in – 'making love') or create a discordant cacophony between you that repels you, and of course the broad spectrum of possibilities in between.

This dynamic of chemistry also means you cannot always 'blame' the other for what gets created and you experience in a situation, as your energy contributes to it too. However, once you get to know your own vibration well, you can generally have a good awareness of what belongs to you and is generally coming from the other source!

And don't discount how strongly the apparently 'subtle' vibration of something can affect how you feel. Aside from the pronounced examples I gave at the beginning of this section, I'll also never forget as a child watching a documentary with my father about people who are deaf and seeing how they could still tap on the beats and rhythm of music that was played to them! I remember asking my dad to explain how that could be so, and he explained they can still feel the vibration of the music hit their body so tangibly! So it's very real.

In my life, I realised I'd often been trying to 'wish away' the impact that some people were having on me, for example if I didn't feel so good in someone's company, I could try to 'think' positively about it, but at the end of the day, their radiance would elicit a particular response as it hit my body.

So rather than fighting this, I started to accept it and trust my instincts in relation to it. This would also work in reverse: sometimes I would be around someone I was attracted to, which another part of my mind would also try and fight sometimes, but ultimately accepting my instincts was more helpful! Again, practising lots of free-form dance like 5Rhythms is incredibly helpful in becoming more aware of your instincts around other people as you can observe the natural inclination of your body. And when you practise it a lot, you build that increased awareness of what your body is saying to you when you are off the dance floor too!

And of course, it was the same with places – I might try and put some mental level spin, interpretation or judgement on how a place presented – usually visually – as good or bad and try to ignore the reality of how it would make me *feel* as its vibration would engage me.

I went through this very process about a holistic health clinic I used to work in that was slightly run-down visually. Of course while its appearance does have importance, I made the mistake of leaving the clinic based primarily on what I thought of its appearance, while choosing to almost completely ignore how great and creative I felt every time I worked there, as the energies and radiance of the building interacted well with me!

So beware the smaller, judgemental, mischievous mind getting in the way of something that feels whole and creative!

The feeling of oneness, of being whole, being in
love is the expression of where those attributes within us
are met wholly by the world around us; the universe and the
dynamic interplay between the two is allowed to flourish.

One cannot find this state of being through pushing
or holding back; then there is separation, the work of
the mischievous mind. It actually depletes our own energies
and resources to push or hold back, a bit like pushing
against a wave or trying not to let go into the flow of it.

When we are in love we can do anything; it describes an ecstatic
state of dynamic equilibrium with the world around us. From
stacking shelves to making love, the missing ingredient is that it
be your path, and when it's your path it will permeate all.
Richard Brook, 2005

And at this time, it also started to dawn on me that it's not just about how other people and objects can influence me, but of course what I'm radiating will also affect other people and things around me too – so best keep myself in good shape on a subtle level, and not get too heavy!

My connection in particular with the Native American tradition also informed me a great deal about interconnection.

While I only write with certainty and authority about things I feel I've got my own realised, embodied understanding of, my experiences engaging with Native American tradition, practices and their ceremonies mean I do also implicitly trust the intelligence of their wise men and women.

And sometimes the Native American awareness of how interconnection works goes so far beyond my own conscious awareness it's truly a wonder to behold, and I feel it's worth sharing some examples that often sit in my mind.

I've participated in Sun Moon Dances for over 20 years – it's a ceremony where you dance for three days without food and water – which were originally brought over to the Western world by the Native American Visionary Beautiful Painted Arrow Joseph Rael. And I remember being told at one dance that the interconnected impact of your dance on the world is that it can actually cause several more people to fall pregnant in the world than would otherwise happen!

And sometimes, while you are dancing, you don't always know or realise what or where the impulse of your dance is created by – it could have a causal link, benefitting or being influenced by other people who may be in other countries even. This is why, ultimately, those dances are about creating world peace, as when you open your awareness, you can connect to the entire universal and planetary consciousness and do your part in transforming some of the density and pain that exists all around us.

**For more on Sun Moon Dances, please visit this blog:
Sun Moon Dance[v]**

---

v   www.creativewellness.co.uk/bookblogs

For more incredibly detailed awareness of the interconnected nature of all, I would suggest reading Beautiful Painted Arrow Joseph Rael's book, *Being and Vibration*[8]. There is a very striking example in that book where he mentions his awareness of how a particular illness a member of their community has actually helps create healing in another part of the universe. It's remarkable reading.

Nuts and Bolts: Tutorial

Vibration

KEY POINT

Every phenomenon within the universe is made up of vibration, including of course you. Things that have a denser, slower vibration tend to be of a more solid nature, such as the body and objects we consider 'solid', like a rock. Things that have a lighter, faster vibration tend to be less tangible, more etheric in nature - such as thoughts or air.

As a human being therefore you have a range of vibrations all the way through from slower, more dense ones which create your tangible physiology, through to less tangible ones which create your emotions and thoughts.

We've all stood next to someone and instinctively realised that they give off a good vibration ('vibe') that may resonate with us and be attractive, or give off vibes that are less appealing, which generally we instinctively move away from.

This is of course also true of places: some places we just like the 'vibe' of, and others not; sometimes we walk into a room and just sense it has a good feeling, or dislike the feeling and can't wait to get out!

So, both animate and inanimate matter can equally influence us, and vice versa, in the sense that our own vibration can also impact other people, and impact inanimate objects too. For example, jewellery, clothing and other objects can pick up the vibrational imprint of the wearer.

How we experience and recognise vibration

The best way to recognise the importance and tangible effect of vibration on our being is through using music as an example. Music is a quite tangible manifestation of vibrations that we can readily relate to. Going back to basics, sounds have particular vibrations which emanate from the instruments or speakers and impact the surrounding matter, in this case you.

So, let's observe what happens when music impacts your body (you don't just hear music through your ears, you actually absorb it and feel it with your whole body). Firstly, you can recognise that certain types of music impact your body in different places – some music makes you feel like moving your hips, some music you may feel opens your heart and puffs your chest out, and some music with a high pitch can feel like it hits you straight between the eyes! If you dance you can also think of how different types of music move you in different ways.

Secondly recognise how you *feel* when different types of music impact your body. Some music energises you like crazy – even when you are in the most sedentary lethargic state you can be moved and exhilarated by particular music – whereas some music has the capacity to relax you to the point you can fall asleep. And some music has the ability to repel you, to make you contract and retreat.

So you can recognise how strongly the vibration of music can move you. However, since everything in existence is made up of vibration, we can also be aware that the body is constantly impacted by vibration that is influencing us.

Think about being within a crowd of people – even if no one is touching you – and think about how that feels, particularly if you are somewhere densely atmospheric like a sports event or concert. And the level of 'sound' you hear is irrelevant. Imagine standing silently with a group of people; that can still be full of vibrational essence strongly hitting the body – often the emotions of the people. Indeed standing in a crowd during a two-minute memorial silence can be incredibly impactful.

Or think of how it feels just before a storm is coming; the atmosphere might be silent where you are, but you feel a tangibly different vibration in the air. Or consider walking into someone else's home on the same street, how it can look the same as your house but can feel so different.

And just the same as with music, all vibration has the capacity to energise, have a neutral impact on the body, or indeed to actually repel you, depending on your own unique vibration profile, as we shall discuss shortly. Similarly, recognise that you also give off vibrations that influence the world around you and whatever you engage with.

How we experience interconnection within the body - chakras

Understanding chakras helps us understand in greater detail how we are influenced by, and influence, what we engage with in the interconnected web of life.

While we feel and radiate vibration through our entire body, it happens, and is filtered particularly through chakras. Chakras are essentially an aggregation of nerves within the body – a nerve 'plexus' – of which we have seven main ones (in the case of the crown chakra it relates to the brain) and aside from the crown and base has openings to the front and back.

They are also sometimes referred to as 'energy centres' (see Image 1).

These energy centres on the body span a spectrum of vibrational frequencies (see Table 1) that relate to the broad spectrum of our human faculties, from our physical body through to our thoughts and feelings and experience of what's around us. They are a big aspect of how we are able to feel, interpret and radiate our experience as a human being. Table 1 also shows several associated functions for each chakra, so you can gain an idea of what may be stimulated in other areas of the body in accordance with the stimulation and function of the chakra too.

KEY POINT

Chakras are not some intangible etheric non-sense; they are each actually grounded within the body itself as they are related to a nerve plexus and are essentially the electromagnetic radiance of that nerve plexus (see Image 1).
This is where the relationship to each chakra having a colour and sound also comes from - different frequencies of electromagnetic energy relate to different colours and sounds. So each different chakra, because it has a different vibrational frequency, has a different colour and sound associated with it.

I will also discuss the important role of chakras in particular in reference to relationship dynamics later, in Chapter 5.

Image 1: Relationship of chakras to
nerve plexuses within the body

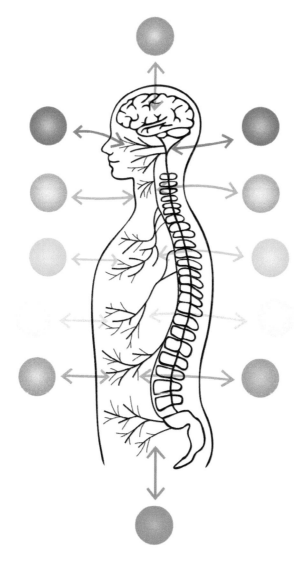

Table 1: Chakra associations[9]

Name	Mooladhara	Swadhisthana	Manipura	Anahata	Vishuddhi	Ajna	Sahasrara
Common name	Root chakra	Sacrum/sacral chakra	Solar plexus chakra	Heart chakra	Throat chakra	Third eye chakra	Crown chakra
Location	Base of spine, sacral plexus	Genitals, fluids	Navel	Heart area	Laryngeal plexus	Between the eyebrows	Top/crown of head, brain
Physical correspondence	Organs of excretion, adrenals	Gonads, reproductive organs	Pancreas, abdominal organs	Thymus, lungs	Thyroid	Pituitary gland	Pineal gland
Emotional correspondence	Survival, primal instinct	Self-acceptance, emotion, sexual energy	Self-will, mental acuity, sense of identity	Compassion, love, healing	Self-expression, speech	Intuition, extra sensory perception	Divinity, peace, enlightenment
Sense	Smell	Taste	Sight	Touch	Hearing	Sixth sense, higher mind	Beyond sensory
Mantra	Lam	Vam	Ram	Yam	Ham	Aum	
Element	Earth	Water	Fire	Air	Ether	Time	Space
Colour	Red	Orange	Yellow	Green	Blue	Indigo	Violet
Frequency	396hz	417hz	528hz	639hz	741hz	852hz	963hz
Sanskrit symbol meaning	Ambition	Desire	Virtue	Compassion	Reflection	Perception	Realisation
Seat	Primal life force	Creativity	Subconscious emotion, ego, will	Love	Creative expression, communication	Primordial power	Liberation, all power, eternal bliss

Your unique vibrational profile

While vibration is the medium by which a person is influenced by another person or object, the mechanics of how that experience is individualised and differs from one person to another can also be explained via the chakra system.

For example, why is it that two people can stand in front of the same person, or object, and have such a different sensory experience of it? One person attracted, and another repelled?

It's because while we all have seven main chakras as outlined earlier, each person actually has a unique set of chakra characteristics, with inherent vibrations of their own which also influences how they experience vibrations from the world.

This means that no two people ever experience the same situation in exactly the same way. Again, using our musical example, one person might be energised by a vibration from a particular song whereas another person might contract away from exactly the same song. Or for example with seasons – one person might really enjoy the warm embrace of the vibration of summer, whereas another person might feel oppressed by it and wish to withdraw from it as it feels like it creates friction for them.

Vibrational 'chemistry' and dynamics

However, it's not quite as simple as your own vibration being 'fixed' to a certain frequency and then you solely experience the vibrational impact of the other particular person or object. This is down to a magical phenomenon that we often refer to as 'chemistry'. We often think of chemistry, or the vibrational 'dynamic' in relation to what happens in relationships with other people, but it can actually be applicable to any situation.

Chemistry refers to what can happen when different sets of vibrations meet that actually create something separate that is then experienced by the contributors, almost as if what you actually experience is seemingly beyond the sum of its parts.

Essentially, as vibrations interact with you from the outside they react with your own vibration (the chemistry bit) and what you actually experience is the resulting dynamic interaction of the two sets of vibrations – not solely the incoming vibration, but that which has been created by the sets of vibrations interacting, and both people (and the life around) become bathed in that chemistry!

So, for example, Tony is feeling a bit tired but relaxed and walks into the room and meets Jessica, who is also feeling a bit tired and relaxed. However due to their unique chemistry, as soon as their vibrations interact with one another, it actually creates a state of feeling energised which they both then experience.

Tony then keeps walking and meets Emily, who is also feeling tired and relaxed but when their energy fields interact the chemistry is different and neither person feels particularly moved by the experience!

The same principle applies to how objects or places can make different people feel different too; to one person a place could have energising chemistry, but to another it could be draining.

The subtlest vibration of all

KEY POINT

Some vibration is so subtle, it is contained within every facet of creation. This is a very high frequency of light which is within all, which is unconditional love.

A moment of unconditional love is a moment where you are a witness of creation without any personality judgement – since in that moment you are connected to something that passes through everything, it cannot be judged, as basically in that moment you are everything! So when you are 'making love' you are actually tuning into a frequency that is at the centre of creation itself!

And making love isn't necessarily a sexual act – 'making love' can happen in many ways. Two people hugging on a street can 'make love'. Two or more people singing a ballad or even rock song together can make love and a whole globe of conscious, aware people with a heartfelt intent could make the hugest amount of love you could possibly imagine! You simply have to open to a frequency that is already in all of us, and accessing this vibration is incredibly nourishing to the soul; it's the seat of all creation. Be it.

Modern-day quantum theory also recognises the interconnection on an atomic level of all creation, so since love is a vibration contained within all matter, when you feel it, it also stimulates it in others through the interconnected resonance[10]. Enjoy!

The range of vibrational interconnection between people and nature

I mentioned earlier how we have seven chakras that span the full range of human faculties, from what's more solid such as the body itself, to our mind and thoughts. Vibrational excitement, harmony, neutrality or friction can actually happen anywhere on the spectrum of the seven chakras.

For example, being in close proximity around a friend, you may pick up and feel their vibration deeply in your physical body, creating an impact on how you physically feel, in your belly, in your legs.

Whereas with another friend, at a greater distance, perhaps even thousands of miles away, they might send out a particular vibration, a particular frequency that you can experience on the most subtle of levels of them appearing in your mind as you 'thinking' about them.

This connection over vast distances with one specific person is also explained by quantum theory, which identifies that once we have been in contact with someone, on an atomic level there can be a kind of 'unconditional bond' created, where basically your atoms become entangled with one another, and this bond actually spans an infinite amount of space, so distance is no object in the resonance of particles with one another.

The interconnection of the planet and universe as a whole

We live as part of a giant ecosystem, where elements are constantly moving about to balance and counterbalance one another. We can see this in a macro sense with the seasons, where in temperate climates it's evident how the seasons balance each other. But even moving beyond the more temperate climates, we can see how across the planet as a whole the vast arid deserts are balanced by the frozen North and South Poles. And think of the other vast ecosystems of plant and animal life, where for billions of years life has acted instinctively and with intelligence to enable it to thrive.

Identifying with this enables us to get a sense of some of the forces acting on us, and understand what they are 'asking' us to do with some faith that there is an intelligence behind them. I will look at two of these core principles, yin and yang and the Five Elements, in Chapter 4.

Tapping into the blueprint of interconnection

Our capacity for self-awareness allows us to not only witness soul level information about things we as an individual can be doing in our life to thrive, but also to witness the network of interconnection that we are part of and act in accordance.

You may find in meditation or times when the more superficial mind is quieter that you can witness your thoughts, and discern that some of them are part of a vaster interconnected web of life and it's bringing you into resonance with other people, places and activities to keep your balance.

Exercises: Interconnection

Vibration

1. Put on some music, or perhaps even better find a dance floor (so the music can potentially be louder) and notice which parts of your body are moved by the music or where you feel the music hitting your body. Also notice the emotional resonance of the music; how does it make you *feel*? If you aren't a fan of dancing as we often can associate it with having to learn a form and have rhythm, or happening in more toxic, discordant environments, find a conscious dance class such as 5Rhythms Dance or Movement Medicine, as in these practices it's a 'conscious' setting and you don't need to know steps.

2. Notice how you feel in your body and emotions when you engage with different people, how their vibration engages you.

3. Notice how you feel in your body within different environments, such as at work and while out in nature. If you are in nature, try standing next to a few different things. Stand next to a rock or tree and see how it makes you feel!

Universal intelligence of interconnection

4. Observe how nature is a giant web of interconnection, with each facet of it playing a part in keeping balance. Think of a plant, how it may nourish and provide life to what's around it – from what it germinates, the seeds and fruits it can produce, the animals it can create food for, the CO_2 it produces, even its decomposition, how it all helps to balance the life around it. You can also do the same for a wild animal, where it moves, what it does, how its actions impact the life around it. Remember you are part of natural life.

5. Reflect on occasions (at least three) where you've followed a creative impulse or instinct you've experienced in your mind, that seemingly was outside of your 'comfort zone' and what were the results? You might experience this as a kind of internal 'nagging' where deep in your mind there is a desire to do something, even if other voices in your mind say no. This can be a way of starting to discern the urging and guiding of the universe upon you to keep balance, its way of moving you around the universal 'dance floor'. Remember everything is in a state of change so you sometimes have to move to keep the overall balance.

6. When you find yourself thinking intently about someone, if it's someone you have good rapport with, ask them if they were similarly thinking of you or conscious of your presence in their mind. You can also do this the other way around, and ask someone if they have thought about you today and then reflect if you were also thinking about them during the day.

Love

7. Notice how love is infectious! Remember how you felt and the impact it had on you when you felt love. How did it affect your own behaviour afterwards? Were you gentler with people (and yourself – your own 'inner critic' softened) afterwards?

4

Understanding Nature and Natural Forces

My nature-full journey

Learning that we are governed by forces of nature was one of the biggest, most stellar and significant impacts on my understanding of life and how I operate as a human being. It's also one of the levels of understanding I often impart to my patients in my clinic, and also appears significantly impactful to them. Here I will look at two main ones, yin and yang and the Five Elements.

Part of the problem is that a great deal of us grow up very isolated from the rhythms and patterns of nature around us, particularly if we live in an urban area. The length of your waking day and state of alertness is more likely to be defined by the level of stress you are under, how many emails you have to deal with, or what time your favourite show finishes at night, rather than what time the sun rises and sets.

The overall amount of work you try and cram into your week can similarly be dictated by what you 'think' is possible, necessary and important to get achieved, rather than any sense of natural balance. And the problem with that is that your thoughts tend to operate much more quickly than your body can! Similarly, with the seasons, who ever really thinks of slowing down significantly in winter – just like the rest of natural life does – when you have so much work to cram in before the holidays and to get everything prepared for festivities?

Before I understood nature and natural forces, I only liked to be 'on'. I got rather attached to the version of me when I was in a fully flushed 'yang' phase, full of energy. I saw that people seemingly appeared to like me when I was full of expression and animation. So I started to neglect my basic desire, instinct and need to say 'no' sometimes, thus skewing the inherent rhythm of activity and rest, which until about the age of 15 I'd naturally done pretty well!

This is not a good state of affairs, as at some point the body has to slow down. For me this showed up as periods of fatigue. One time for around a year, my entire body had had enough and 'grounded me' at home.

It was only when I started to study Taoism, and my acupuncture degree, where we spent a great deal of time observing nature and keeping a seasons diary of what we witnessed in natural life around us, that I really started to understand that the inherent balance of activity and rest, expansion and contraction (basically yin and yang) is part of life by design! And indeed, that these phases actually feed into and perpetuate one another.

I finally started to answer the call of going 'inwards' and resting, although that wasn't considered cool in my youth, though who cares if it looks boring to those around me?

Of course it's actually not boring, but I'd developed a value judgement around it at some point, so it's funny that a massive part of what I teach now is the ability to switch off, and it's noticeable how many people around are now actually stressed and desperate to slow down and rest deeply! And I developed the awareness that the more I actually go 'inside', the more my energy actually comes back to the surface with power, potency and vitality when it does.

When I started to become even wiser to it, I realised that what we think of as switching off and relaxing still leaves a lot to be desired. I started to get clued up that the 'switching off' a lot of us do, sitting at home and watching TV, or playing on the laptop or phone, is actually still pretty stimulating, irritating the hypothalamus of the brain and still significantly stimulating the nervous system.

This was where I really started to appreciate the regenerative effect of practices like yoga, meditation and particularly the deep relaxation that you experience at the end of a yoga class. 'Amplified relaxation' I call it. If you have amplified stress in your life, which virtually anyone in an urban environment has, you certainly need amplified relaxation techniques to balance this out, as they take you into a much deeper relaxation response than that glass of red wine while sitting watching your favourite show ever can do!

I started to notice that after the relaxation of my yoga class I would feel so much more refreshed than even after hours of sleep! I actually became much more productive as a result.

I learned to embrace my tiredness, rather than try and fight it, something I still commonly see today. For example in people who are really tired but still hitting the gym – trying to get a short-term buzz off the exercise, but actually still eroding their inner reserves. Think about it; think about when you were a child, and your energy would naturally bubble back up to the surface and want to outwardly express after a rest; you wouldn't need to force it! And then you'd naturally rest when tired.

Now I plan my week and year honouring this balance of yin and yang, and try and honour it in the moment of course too where possible, no more trying to be superman. Being perfectly human is fine for now!

Within this observation of nature, I also saw more than just this singular expansion and contraction, rest and activity. I also started to see the phases that life goes through during this cycling between the polarities of activity to rest.

And this is where I started to understand the Five Elements, the different phases that exist between the extremes of being 'in' and 'out'. Again, just like the seasons around me, I noticed I naturally have an inclination and 'calling' for phases where I'm building like spring, and other phases where I'm letting go like autumn. I'm happier this way, sure in the knowledge that at last I've found an instruction manual of how to pace my life based on being part of nature and its inherent creative intelligence.

Since we use this model of the Five Elements for understanding the nature and tendencies of people themselves, deepening my awareness of the elements was also fundamental to my acceptance of people around me. So instead of judging others (and myself) in accordance with a fixed template of how people *should* be, I appreciated that people had a natural tendency towards different elements within them being dominant, depending on their own constitution. From an acupuncture practitioner perspective this was also a godsend, as then you fully realise that what you are actually trying to do as a practitioner is just make people more of who they naturally are, not what you want them to be!

Nuts and Bolts: Tutorial

You are part of nature

Having learned about the relationship of the soul to our experience in life, and how we interconnect with the world around us, let's consider next the natural laws that regulate our experience on Earth, as we travel in a vehicle – a body – that is dictated to by them. So getting to know them and being friends with them is much better than fighting with them!

My experience tells me that even holistically aware people can often fall down in this understanding of how we also operate within a bigger body of life that strongly affects us. It's essential to realise holistic doesn't just mean what goes on *within* you, your thoughts and feelings, it also means being aware of the influences that are acting on you from the outside and the role you also play within that bigger whole.

For example, just as we have cells within our body that have intelligence to them and support the overall functioning of the body, you can think of it that you, as a whole human being, are also a cell within a bigger body of life, and are under the direction of forces that act on you (such as yin and yang and the Five Elements).

Also consider that if you are just like a 'cell' within the bigger body of the planetary whole, it then also makes sense that you may also be specifically directed by an intelligence to help support the overall balance and functioning of the body around you. Thinking about how 'healer' cells in the body get naturally directed to the site of an injury, also consider that you may be moved and directed to places to bring your natural skills to help others.

KEY POINT

The first idea to get comfortable with is that you are a part of nature by design. It's crucial since you can then begin to understand that, just like nature around you, you are built to be able to move and flow with natural principles and be in balance and harmony with what's around you.

Nature is constantly, moment to moment, seeking to find balance, to find its highest potential! Richard Brook, 2004

Understanding this allows you to shift from thinking that being healthy and balanced is some kind of unwarranted or unlikely fantasy, or an abstract idea, but actually it's your natural birthright. You are not in alignment if you are not in tune with the desire of creation for you to thrive.

Indeed if we have become acclimatised to sheltered urban lifestyles, we can start to think of the natural world as being 'alternative' whereas, of course, nature is indeed our natural habitat! But of course, like any animal that's been domesticated or lived predominantly outside its natural habitat, it can take a while and be a gentle process to be released back into the wild, so we'll go easy! However we learn a lot about how our body and mind operates when we understand we are designed as part of natural life.

Natural patterns

Observe the phenomena of the different seasons. See how they all have unique characteristics but yet seamlessly merge into one another and combine together to create balance across the course of a year. This is the metaphor for how you operate as a human being.

We use the concepts of yin and yang and Five Elements extensively in this book and you can identify both over the course of a yearly cycle. Yin and yang can be used to describe the relative opposites within the year of winter and summer and can also be used to describe the phases of increasing light (a yang phase) between winter and summer solstice and decreasing light (a yin phase) between summer and winter solstices. So sometimes you are really pushing out into the world – yang – and sometimes you are really retreated inwards – yin.

However of course you don't just flip from the extremes of winter to summer and back – you have phases, which we call seasons, which happen between them to complete the entire cycle. Spring, a phase of growth and expansion. Autumn, a period of letting go of old growth to create space for the new. And Chinese medicine also identifies an additional season of late summer, a kind of neutral phase between energy reaching its most outward 'yang' peak in summer and beginning its 'yin' descent into autumn.

And so it's the same in you!

You have phases just like spring where you get an almighty kick of energy to start creating and growing, you have phases just like summer where the heat draws you out to just open and enjoy, phases like late summer, which feel consolidatory and centring, phases like autumn where you shed what you no longer need, and phases like winter where although there is still a lot going on under the surface, you still shut off deeply and head inside!

You can also identify this combination of yin and yang and different elements being present across the life cycle of virtually any phenomena. They can happen across the course of one day, and of course they also happen across the course of the year. Essentially, we can see all around us that quiet and rest gives rise to growth which matures and declines before coming back to rest again.

And staying in tune with these seasonal changes isn't something you have to force, due to our clever human design where different climatic conditions naturally resonate with aspects of our physiology.

In essence seasons move you much like music on a dance floor moves you, as each season has a different vibrational rhythm that actually stimulates particular organs in the body which are responsible for the corresponding quality in you. This elicits particular behaviours and also the ability of those organs to resource themselves on the energy of the season – this is important as each season fuels you up with a certain type of energy that then feeds into the next!

For example the 'Wood' season in nature – spring – draws out the Wood Element in you as it stimulates the liver and gall bladder which comprise the Wood Element within you.

This is why it's important to flow with the energy of the seasons as they present themselves as you can't cheat them or recreate them later! For example, you might notice we have the common notion of a 'summer of love' as the heat stimulates the heart to draw us out to connect with people, but we don't get the idea of a winter of love as by then different organs have taken the ascendancy! And you have to fully live the energy of a season or it will compromise the rest of the cycle – if the trees never shed their old growth in autumn, how could anything grow in spring? There would be no space for anything new and vibrant. So it's exactly the same in your life; compromising one phase will affect the others.

Staying in tune with the seasons

Spring
let yourself be creative and make the plans and structure that allow your year to be amazing.

Summer
enjoy the dropping of layers around your heart as the heat draws you out to connect with life around you.

Late summer
allow yourself to reap the benefits of what you have grown during the year.

Autumn
allow yourself to shed layers on all levels that you no longer need and start to head inside.

Winter
allow yourself to retreat deeply inside, safe in the knowledge things are growing under the surface.

Allowing ourselves to actually flow with these seasonal shifts can be a massive challenge in the way we live our modern lives in that we seem to want to go at exactly the same pace whatever the season is, and also because we measure time in a linear fashion, counting upwards rather than recognising it as cyclical. On the other hand, if you allow the seasonal energy to take you on the ride we have outlined above you will stay in more robust health.

To pass fully through the five enables us to stay as ONE.
Richard Brook, 2005

Going deeper: Yin and Yang

Yin and yang is one of those concepts that crops up often in yoga and natural therapies and the intelligence of what it represents is indeed profound.

The principles of yin and yang describe how "seemingly opposite or contrary forces may actually be complementary, interconnected and interdependent in the natural world, and how they may give rise to each other as they interrelate to one another"[11]. *(Thanks to Wikipedia for that definition; couldn't have said it any better myself!)*

Image 2: Yin yang symbol

In essence they are two phases that comprise and radiate through any aspect of our being. Think of the universe as one whole mass of creation which can then break down into various divisions with the first division splitting it into two which creates the yin and yang aspects. Or think of how the 24 hours of a day can be seen as one unit, but can then also be broken down into daytime and night time. Or humans can be seen as one species, but within it you have male and female and so on.

And when we divide up any entity into two, we assign those new elements into yin or yang categories depending on their *relative* characteristics (see Table 2).

Table 2: Yin and yang correspondences

Yin	Yang
Winter	Summer
Female	Male
Moon	Sun
Contracting	Expanding
Inward	Outward
Downward	Upward
Introvert	Extrovert

However, what's really important to note is that yin and yang categorisations aren't absolute, as they are describing the characteristics of two things *relative* to one another. For example, England's weather is yin (cooler) compared to Spain's yang (hotter) weather. But Spain's weather would be yin (cooler) compared to Mexico's yang (hotter) weather. Or in a yogic sense, the Dru yoga I teach is yin (gentle and slow) compared to Ashtanga yoga's (stronger and faster) yang. But the Dru I teach would be yang compared to Restorative yoga which is even more gentle and slower.

**For more on yin and yang please visit this blog:
Yin & Yang and The Forces of Nature[vi]**

Why does yin and yang affect life on planet earth?

The reason that yin and yang forces operate so clearly through our natural world on this planet is due in part to sunlight. The sun is a massive yang force, providing heat and light that catalyses movement and animation from the natural life that it influences. We can see this across the course of a day: as your part of the planet moves into position to be exposed to the sun, so it creates movement and animation in the life under it – we get up and move out into the world. And then as the amount of light falls, so natural life retreats back to rest.

You can also clearly identify this influence of sunlight across the course of a year: as the sun increases there is more growth, and as it decreases after summer solstice natural life goes into decay, decline and rest in order to replenish for the next year.

So all living matter, including human beings, is subjected to natural forces of expansion and contraction, activity and rest, and growth and decay.

Our original 'blueprint'

When we are younger we tend to naturally be more in tune with the inherent flow of the cycles we have been discussing – such as with the daily and seasonal cycles, and the ability to balance outward movement with rest. However, as we develop in life the various cultural and societal forces that

---

vi   www.creativewellness.co.uk/bookblogs

act upon us (the stresses and strains of modern life which run counter-current to our natural tendencies) start to skew this balance, creating stress within our system that can lead to imbalance. And our 'inner navigation' and attunement to these natural patterns also becomes jumbled, and can need correction.

The chart on the following page, 'Balance and Imbalance: Path of Division', illustrates this dynamic relationship between the forces of nature and what goes on within the body, seen from the Taoist and Chinese medicine perspective of elements, meridian and (acupuncture) points, and how they can come out of balance when we lose connection to natural rhythms.

Similarly, the image on page 78 also depicts various aspects and dynamics of our path of division and how existence is One before manifesting in many levels and layers.

The image initially started out as just the flame in the centre, with the blue streaks indicating heavier and denser energy that gets dispersed when the light becomes brighter and more intense within us. I identify this Light as the one light that illumines all, the pure light which exists at source and from which all creation derives, begins and ends. The blue streaks are erroneous energies which 'get in the way' of our connection and expression of this source or Light – or energetic blocks which are an aspect of who we are as people, but which we can polish or shine whilst incarnated. We do this by allowing that Light through, or attuning to it (please see Chapter 7, What happens when you meditate or tune into a healing energy).

Balance and Imbalance
Path of Division

Energy is constantly seeking to find balance, to find its highest potential.

Within the whole 'one' mass of energy which comprises the universe, each and every one of us has a space, a path, where being in tune with our path and our environment means we shall ride a wave through the cycles of the one, through the undulations of the one through expansion and contraction, movement and stillness, through the seasons and cycles.

ILL HEALTH AND DISEASE ALL COMES FROM SPLITTING FROM THE ONE, OUR ONE

First you'll divide from the undulations between expansion and contraction, a division from the two phases of yin and yang within the one

Thus our yin and yang will need rebalancing

Next you'll divide and separate from the journey of the Five Elements (seasons) within the one, thus our Five Elements will need rebalancing

Within this you will divide from the journey of the 12 phases (months) within the one, thus our 12 meridians will need rebalancing

Within this you will divide from the journey of the 365 phases (days) within the one, thus our 365 points will need rebalancing

****

However **EVERYTHING IS CONNECTED:**
Imbalance at the level of the 365 can cause imbalance at the level of the one,
That is why the Earth is round
Richard Brook, 2005

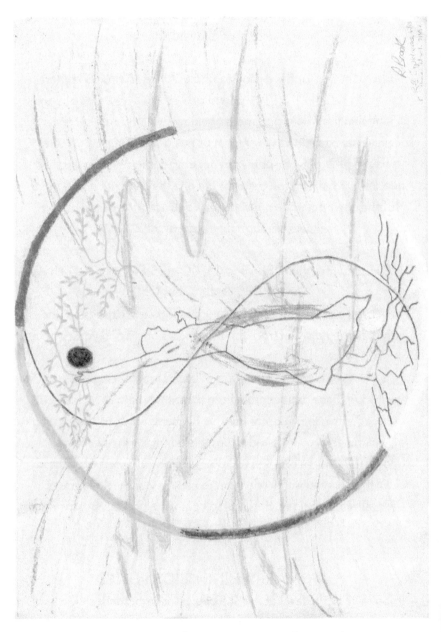

Image 3: Everything we are comes from Light

Interestingly, I drew the 'Light' part of the image after visioning it whilst meditating at the Cluny Hill site of the Findhorn Foundation intentional community in Scotland where I lived for a while. It's notable as I later found out, many years later from reading the autobiography of Peter Caddy (one of the founders of the Foundation), that they had been guided while at Cluny Hill to establish it as a 'Centre of Light' and over many years 'built up the Light' there.[12]

Later I added the yin and yang symbolism, as I began to understand that yin and yang represent that One single solitary Light energy as it divides down between its phases of contraction and expansion, outwards and inwards movement. The greater the extent we flow with this, generally the more healthy we are.

And then you have the representation of the third division which is Heaven, Earth and Hu(Man)ity. This is shown by the tree branches growing upwards and out of the man's hands towards the sky, and the roots from the feet into the Earth, and how in balance as people we walk between these two forces – enough connection to the Heavens and Spirit to take inspiration but also grounded and rooted enough to get things done on Earth.

Finally, around the man in the circle are five different colours, which represent the 5 Elements phases of expansion and contraction which we all pass through during a day, year and lifetime! Green represents our Wood Element of growth, red our Fire Element of maturation, yellow our Earth Element of consolidation or equipoise/neutrality, white our Metal Element of decline/letting go and blue our Water Element of stillness. The image has a lot of meaning for me as the silhouette is also taken from a photo of me dancing that

I traced around! So every level aspect of the image strongly connects for me.

The internal mechanics - how your body keeps you attuned to yin and yang

In order to keep attuned to this natural flow of inward and outward movement we therefore have organs within the body which drive the 'yang', outward movement and growth, and organs within the body which bring us back inwards into 'yin' movement to rest and restore. This is how we are naturally designed as part of the matrix of natural life.

So if we overdo the outward movement, it not only strains the 'yang' organs, but it also depletes the 'yin' organs trying to replenish us. The occasional excess we can cope with, but it's when we develop a chronic pattern of overwork and stress (a massive dis-ease in the Western world) then we start to develop problems.

For example, we can sleep off the occasional excess, have a few extra hours' rest (as we would as a child), but over a longer period of time the body develops a pattern of being overdriven, becomes tight, restless ('rest-less') and starts to compensate using adrenal energy (fight or flight) which we should really only be using in times of genuine alarm and emergency! We then become chronically tired.

And since all organs within the body are interconnected, it's not just one organ – or 'element' – within us that suffers. Using our seasonal analogy, if one season within the course of the year is way off balance then the following seasons can also suffer, and the overall whole balance is compromised.

As an example of the knock-on effect of overwork, as

your adrenals overactivate, it depletes your kidney energy. This adrenal overactivation also catalyses a decrease in digestive efficiency as your body feels under threat so starts to shut down on what it considers less essential systems (you'll keep breathing, but the body feels it can compromise digestion in this instance), and this affects your stomach and spleen. In this pattern the liver often starts to get hot as it has more work to do than normal to hold structure and push through action which in turn also makes us lose our appetite, not to mention affecting sleep and making us irritable. And this heat in turn radiates up and underneath the heart, making us blow things out of proportion and our emotions erratic.

Conversely, if we don't move enough and become too yin, spend too much time being sedentary, then the yang organs responsible for movement and animation become stagnant, a bit like water that's sat too long, which develops a layer of sediment distancing it from the world so it needs shaking up and refreshing to become energised again. And similarly, there will be a knock-on effect throughout the rest of the organs and elements. The state of stagnation can affect the spontaneity and animation of the heart; it dampens the ability of the liver to assert itself and have clarity of vision for the future and so on.

So as you can see, it's never just one level of us that gets affected; an excess in one aspect of our life will in turn affect others. There are only 24 hours in a day; if you spend too much time in excessive work and stress, by its very nature it compromises the time available to feed and resource ourselves, to socialise and pursue new interests and adventures. If you spend too much time without movement, animation and assertion then it compromises the time available to be growing in your life.

What can happen for a lot of us as we age and move into less healthy lifestyle patterns is that the naturally strong polarity of yin and yang becomes compromised. So, once we may have had a very clear division between the body in motion, activity, assertion, and then an equally clear polarity of the body in rest. Again, think of a child: the sun comes up and the child naturally gets activated and moves out into the world, then with nightfall the sleep is as deeply engaged as the daytime activity was. So there is a very strong polarity between activity and rest.

However, a lot of modern lifestyles dictate that our daytime work can be sedentary. Thus our 'yang' organs don't get sufficient expression, and then when the yin organs try and take ascendancy in the evening we are agitated and restless as the yang organs are still activated, which still calls our attention outside. This isn't helped by phones, TVs and the plethora of modern-day urban distractions and this often means that even when we sleep the yang organs and nervous system are still overstimulated, resulting in disturbed sleep and in turn further depleting the yin organs.

When we are younger the organs more spontaneously bounce back from overexertion, but the passage of time and the phenomenon of the circadian rhythm of the body (that the body moves in a 24-hour cycle) lends itself to the organs getting stuck in patterns. These patterns can continue long past the time the original external stimulus might have ceased.

The body's circadian rhythm means that this pattern then continues on again the next day too, and so on, with organs being chronically stressed and stuck in patterns of overstimulation even after the stimulation has long gone! Think about how sometimes it can take such a long time to 'unwind'. A mild example of this is when people go on holiday and it takes them days to relax. In severe examples people stay anxious and restless for indefinite periods of time, particularly if the stimulation was tending towards being traumatic.

So this is where skilled therapeutic support can be helpful as sometimes these patterns are so deeply ingrained into the body that they manifest as what we call 'energy blocks' – where organs just can't switch off to relax and it creates imbalanced relationships between organs. This is something we treat a lot in acupuncture – and fatigue states can also often result from this pattern within the body.

All the above might sound complicated, but in a lot of ways it's actually not – the solution is always to realign back to your instincts which are ALWAYS there. Nature is always seeking to find balance. Often you just need help in coming back to your instincts and senses and undoing some of the knots in the mind and misguided beliefs which you have developed to suppress them.

As a practitioner and teacher this is what I'm always trying to achieve for my patients – to bring you back to your own higher awareness of what you need.

Helpful therapies and activities

We'll detail therapies in greater depth in Chapter 7, but it's useful to consider some broad recommendations in relation to yin and yang.

If you are yang excessive and thus yin deficient (this is

most of us in the Western world to some degree as we are generally overstimulated) then it's where yin activities like yoga and meditation are useful, since you will need amplified 'yin' activities to calm and balance your nervous system and organs in a much more concentrated way. Walks in nature can also be particularly soothing.

As I've said, different organs can become stuck in a circadian rhythm pattern which can take a while to 'unwind' from and acupuncture can be tremendous at supporting specific organs in this way. With the converse, where yin is in excess and yang deficient, again yoga and acupuncture can be wonderful at freeing up energy that has become stuck or stagnant, as can regular energising physical activities, giving the body a kick start to resetting the circadian rhythm.

Working with the balance of the body on this level is the purpose of traditional acupuncture, as opposed to more modern medical, Western, or 'dry needling' acupuncture, which tends to work on more symptomatic or musculoskeletal levels.

The mental level

With a state of yin deficiency and yang excess, it's worth noting that it can often be accompanied by a great deal of mental disquiet, with the mind racing, as there is a lack of internal calm and a degree of agitation. This can actually make engaging with quieter and more 'yin' activities feel a little uncomfortable as it can seem to bring our awareness even more to our internal disquiet and racing mind. Despite this sense of discomfort, it's actually a sign that you need to relax your nervous system even more to restore balance.

Therefore gentle activities which can still involve some

movement, such as walking, spontaneous dance or yoga, can be good in this circumstance as they still allow the body to burn off some of the internal yang (agitation) while still nourishing the yin. However, it's essential not to 'push' as that just defeats the object.

With a yin excess and yang deficiency, the mental state can be a sense of resistance to change, as energy is stuck, congealed and doesn't want to move. Therefore activities and exercises which move the body relatively quickly – faster than the mind can catch up and complain – can be helpful!

The microcosmic orbit

The microcosmic orbit exercise can also help you to balance your internal yin and yang. It's a meditation exercise where you trace your awareness up the 'Du' channel, which is the body's most prominent yang energy channel which runs up the spine, and down the 'Ren' channel which is the body's most prominent yin channel which runs down the front of the body, together forming a complete circuit. The technique is described in the exercises.

For more on the microcosmic orbit please visit this blog: The Microcosmic Orbit - Balance Your Yin and Yang[vii]

---

vii   www.creativewellness.co.uk/bookblogs

Exercises: Yin and yang

1. Have a look at the yin and yang principle in your life – is the overall structure of your life set up to even give you a chance to balance your yin and yang? How much time and space for rest do you have built in, alongside working and socialising and other activities that take you out into the world?

2. Look at the specific polarities of yin and yang in your life. Write down the activities that strongly assert your yang, that really rev your body up and get it moving, where you are really expressing your energy actively and outwardly. And write down the activities in your life that equally as deeply switch your body off, that allow you to rest deeply.

3. The microcosmic orbit

Place your awareness in your perineum (midway between the anus and vaginal opening on females, midway between the anus and testicles on males) and as you breathe in, trace your awareness up your spine to the top of your head. You are following the Du channel, the main yang energy pathway in the body. As you breathe out, continue tracing your awareness straight down the front of the head, neck and body back to the perineum. Now you are following the Ren channel, the main yin channel. Place your tongue behind your teeth in the roof of your mouth to complete the energetic circuit.

Bringing your awareness through the channels in this way helps to rebalance your natural polarity of yin and yang and your energy body.

Practise this regularly for 5–10 minutes and notice how you feel afterwards. You can do it while sitting or standing and once it's created an established pattern in your mind you can switch it on or off at will, even while busy, as a means of regaining balance.

Going deeper: Getting to know the five elements

In a similar way to how we likened yin and yang to being the entirety of creation split into two aspects, the Five Elements can be seen as the entirety of creation divided into five aspects. Keeping our seasonal analogy we see can see the Five Elements as being like the seasons within the year, the phases that happen within the overall cycle of growth (yang) and decay (yin). Identifying the elements as having similar qualities to the seasons is also a very good way of becoming familiar with their characteristics.

Table 3: Five Elements correspondences

The Five Elements	Corresponding season	Corresponding organs	Quality
Wood	Spring	Liver & gall bladder	Yang
Fire	Summer	Heart, small intestine, pericardium, triple heater*	Yang
Earth	Late summer	Spleen & stomach	Neutral
Metal	Autumn	Lung & large intestine	Yin
Water	Winter	Kidney & bladder	Yin

*As an exception, the Fire Element, rather than having two organs, contains four organs one of which, the triple heater, is a function of the heart without having a physical structure as such.

The crucial point is that the Five Elements aren't just an abstract concept, they are relatable to all of creation – just like yin and yang. Therefore the corresponding qualities can be seen in a human being all the way through from our behavioural traits to a pair of organs within the body.

Your internal organs are the host for your elements

The organs within your body host, express, and keep the balance for the different elements within you and what you need to stay happy and healthy. When the organs are out of balance, or our lifestyle is negatively impacting them, it can affect our balance in life. Essentially we need to do all we can in our lives to give each element the supportive circumstances it needs to thrive.

The context of 'organs'

In the strictest sense, although I am directly referring to 'organs' there's actually a broader phenomenon than the physical structure of the organ itself that I am discussing. The named organ also relates to a system of meridians (pathways of energy – from the Chinese medicine system) which are also connected to that organ, and also encompasses a fuller spectrum of physical, mental, emotional and spiritual capacities. Indeed, in Five Elements theory, each organ is sometimes referred to as an 'official' to give due respect to this broader range of capacities.

So in the following chapters when I discuss being aware of the expression of the organs either externally in your behaviour, or internally in your mind, you can frame it in the broader context of the meridian system and that the organ can be communicating across a spectrum from its very visceral, physical need, through to its more spirit level need.

For example, when you interpret your stomach being hungry and wanting more nourishment, it can be on that very physical level that you need to eat, and sometimes it can be on the more etheric spirit level of communication that your soul is hungry for more enriching experience.

Your elements are also the vehicle of expression for your soul

You can also therefore incorporate the understanding that in the broadest sense each organ and element is actually host to an aspect of your soul. Essentially organs provide the physical vehicle that allows different aspects of your soul to play out their path and destiny here on Earth, and since the organs and elements are aligned to the laws of nature they provide some form that we have to adhere to in order to maintain balance.

Your unique elemental profile

It's important to understand that although each of us has all the elements within, and we move between the expression of them in order to keep balance (just like the cycle of the seasons), the school of thought in Five Elements theory is that you actually have a hierarchy of the elements with one predominant one.

So one person may have a tendency towards more Fire characteristics, another more Wood characteristics and so on. This unique elemental profile will influence an entire spectrum from the quality of energy within the corresponding organs to emotional expression, tendencies and behaviours.

So by observing key physical, mental, emotional and behavioural correspondences in yourself and others it can give an indication as to the elemental balance, and increase self-awareness about your own unique characteristics.

Physiological correspondences

Each element comes with a number of specific physiological correspondences, for example the Fire Element is also related to blood vessels, the Wood Element to ligaments and tendons, the Earth Element to muscles and so on. But the elements can also be identified by what we refer to as colour, sound, odour and emotion (CSOE).

These are observable signs of each element on the physical level. For example, the CSOE of the Wood Element are green, shouting, rancid and anger. This means that someone with a Wood Element in excess could present with a green hue on the face, an audible shouting quality in the voice, a smell of rancidity and an emotion of anger. Or conversely a deficient Wood Element could see a distinct lack or absence of all these qualities – less apparent green, a timid voice, no rancid smell, and again a timid emotional disposition.

Each element has its own individual CSOE which we will outline below, and observing them can be a good way of becoming conscious of which elements are more prominent in you.

As a Chinese medicine acupuncture practitioner, it's these *sensory* signs that I take into account when I diagnose and treat patients as it gives me an indication of the underlying organ function much more clearly than intellectual content does. By this I mean that 10 people could all have the same condition or illness as recognised in Western medicine, but from the Chinese medicine perspective each of those people would have a unique treatment prescribed for them as the subtle condition of their organs would all be totally unique to them, as indicated by the CSOE.

Elements are also observable internally, through your self-awareness

While it's useful to become aware of some of the 'exterior' characteristics of your elements, a stellar leap in personal development happens when you become more internally aware and discerning of the expression of the intelligence of the Elements within you directly in each moment.

This enables you to start to understand and recognise your unique qualities and expressions, rather than just physically 'diagnose' yourself. This is possible as you can prime your internal awareness and senses in just the same way as you can prime your external awareness and senses, and begin to interpret the 'inner' voice of the elements, literally how you experience and hear them in your mind. This is important as external physical signs and signals of our elemental state can be more chronic and may not necessarily give us direct feedback of what we need right now, in this moment.

We will examine this inner experience of the elements in greater detail in Chapter 5.

The descriptions below give a more detailed breakdown of some of the key characteristics of each element.

Wood Element

Organs: Liver and gall bladder
Wood is nourished by asserting your life path into the world, being flexible where necessary and asserting where necessary (and not overloading your liver with toxic relationships – from substances or people).

Associated colour, sound, odour and emotion (these can be particularly prominent or diminished in a person's expression depending on whether there is an excess or deficiency of the element)

Colour – Green
Sound – Shout
Odour – Rancid
Emotion – Anger/assertion

Behaviourally and emotionally
People with a more pronounced Wood Element may have a strong and clear vision for the future and be able to assert themselves clearly and forcefully, make fixed plans, or at the other end of the spectrum may lack clarity and vision, be unable to assert very well, lack plans and struggle with decisions.

Supportive season – spring
You may find yourself making more plans at this time of the year and creating the structure for the growth that's coming ahead, just as nature creates new growth and new branches at this time.

Fire Element

Organs: Heart, small intestine, pericardium and triple heater

To be nourished the Fire Element needs connection to your passions in life, healthy relationships, joy, connection to your soul or higher consciousness (as it resides in the heart).

Associated colour, sound, odour and emotion

Colour – Red
Sound – Laugh
Odour – Scorched
Emotion – Joy

Behaviourally and emotionally

People with a more pronounced Fire Element may find themselves strongly focused on their passions since heart and passions are so closely linked with a particular focus on their relationships, since by nature they are also affairs of the heart! They can suffer with issues around excess or deficiency of joy – they may be predominantly jovial even when inappropriate, or always low. Fire also tends to express through how animated someone is – comedians tend to have a predominant Fire energy as so much of their disposition is targeted towards animation, laughter and joy. A general lack of animation can be a sign of a depleted Fire Element, or that it doesn't rank very highly in your elemental hierarchy.

Supportive season – summer

You may find yourself reaching out to connect with others more at this time of year, shedding layers both in terms of your actual physical clothing but also the layers you place around your heart as the sun draws you out.

Earth Element

Organs: Stomach and spleen
To be nourished requires nurture, support from home and family life, sustenance, stability.

Associated colour, sound, odour and emotion

Colour – Yellow
Sound – Sing
Odour – Fragrant
Emotion – Sympathy

Behaviourally and Emotionally
People with a more pronounced Earth Element may find themselves more strongly focused on the securities of life – having a settled home, eating well, looking after themselves and their regular patterns. They also have a strong compassionate streak – playing 'mother' to others. At the other end of the spectrum, they may suffer with a deficiency of all of the above – struggling to feel settled and nourished, lack of compassion to others, etc.

Supportive season – late summer
You may find yourself really reaping the benefits of what you have created so far this year, enjoying the fruits of your labour!

Metal Element

Organs: Lung and large intestine

To be nourished requires time in an expansive environment (out of the normal routine) to facilitate perspective (amplifying lung energy), removing clutter and keeping things in order.

Associated colour, sound, odour and emotion

Colour – White
Sound – Weep
Odour – Rotten
Emotion – Grief

Behaviourally and emotionally

People with a more pronounced Metal Element, again on a spectrum of excess or deficiency, may find themselves more strongly focused around connection to the whole (as air binds through everything), feeling inspired (or lack of), maintaining a broader perspective on things, clarity and tidiness of the space around you, needing to let go of things, obsession with being clear, neat and tidy, having things to throw away or collecting and hoarding, and grief (or lack of).

Supportive season – autumn

You may find yourself with a new sense of clarity and space and inspiration at this time of year, as old memories from the past begin to fall away, much as the trees start to get rid of their old growth.

Water Element

Organs: Kidney and bladder

Water is nourished by rest (quieting the kidneys and adrenals and allowing them to rebalance), reflection, flowing with your destiny – applying your willpower to what's in your heart.

Associated colour, sound, odour and emotion

> Colour – Blue
> Sound – Groan
> Odour – Putrid
> Emotion – Fear

Behaviourally and emotionally

People with a more pronounced Water Element may find themselves more strongly oriented to be being 'driven' or having a lack of 'drive' in life, have tendencies towards fear or lack of fear, be reflective or have an aura of wisdom (or again lack of) and may either be strong and robust or somewhat withdrawn at times (to conserve energy).

Supportive season – winter

You may find yourself heading 'inwards' into introspection and reflection as the energy of the kidney and bladder pull you into the most 'yin' and internal aspect of your being – in the same way the growth in nature at this time of year is happening deep under the surface, with at the top a sense of stillness.

The Five Elements in common awareness

It's worth noting how in our everyday language we have somehow already made associations between particular organs and their corresponding qualities and influence on our body, mind and spirit.

For example, we call people who can't assert themselves 'lily livered' or conversely those who over-assert we reference as having a 'lot of gall'. This obviously associates to the Wood Element of liver and gall bladder and how it relates to the spectrum of assertion.

Or we call people who are excessively clean, neat and tidy 'anal', making the obvious association to the role of the large intestine in this behaviour.

How the elements relate to areas of your life

Since each element within the body has certain qualities, needs and dispositions, we can also broadly identify which area of your life and tendencies they relate to. Indeed, within the previous section I mentioned several times practical things that we may also be doing which could be upsetting each element – occupations, relationships, nutrition and so on.

It's important to note, however, that in some respects these are broad correspondences as we can also see that an element can relate to multiple areas of your life. As an example, to have a successful career that you enjoy and feel passionate about requires your Fire Element to be engaged which relates to joy and your heart, and similarly, of course, to have a loving, caring, passionate relationship requires your Fire Element to be engaged!

However, it's an interesting exercise to broadly map out the areas of your life that each element mainly corresponds to, since if that area of your life is discordant, it will either be negatively affecting the element, stressing it, or it could be an indicator of an inherent imbalance in the element within you which is manifesting outwardly within that area of your life.

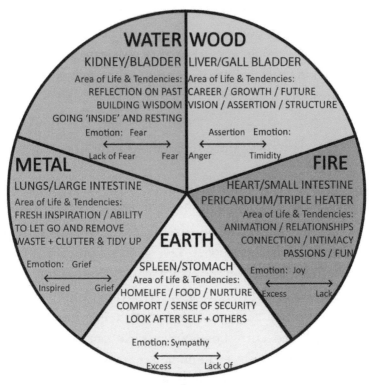

Image 4: The Five Elements of your life

Notes on the lifestyle manifestation of your elements

Wood Element: Creates the vision and applies the decisions to create growth in your life, so your occupations are a reflection of this. This commonly includes our job; since we spend so much time at work, the Wood Element often takes command of how we are choosing to spend our time. However, it might well show through hobbies or interests that are growing on the side or your work, or if you are in a situation where your job is a bit of an immovable object! The underlying point is there will be a vision and application to create growth in your life.

Fire Element: Tends to show in your passions, whether that's with other people, relationships or again your work. If you aren't passionate about anything you do, then your Fire Element is diminished.

Earth Element: The ability to look after your basic needs – so it will show in your home life, how good you are at making a nest for yourself, feeding and looking after yourself.

Metal Element: Your ability to 'let go' and create space. It often reflects in how much clutter you have around you in your life, either physical clutter, how much old 'stuff' you have lying around or how clean you keep the space. (Remember it inhibits growth if too much old stuff is lying around as it blocks the new – think about the autumn tree analogy and the need to shed the leaves – it blocks the light and space for new things to grow if the old leaves don't fall away.)

Water Element: Will show in how much time and space you leave for yourself to go inwards, and how comfortable you are in doing so! If you are always busy, then you're not leaving enough time for your Water Element to integrate experiences, to reflect on them and generate new wisdom, so you can tend to not actually progress as quickly in life. Sometimes less is more.

Exercises: The Five Elements

1. Reflect on how you feel your own inner configuration of Five Elements is structured – which do you feel you are most familiar with and are most pronounced, and which are least?
2. Have a look at your life and see if it is structured to feed and nourish all your Five Elements.
3. Start keeping a seasons diary! Make notes of what you see going on around you in nature and how you feel during each season. You will be amazed at how different you can feel so it's good to note the insights so you can keep them in your awareness during subsequent years. Often the variance can be so strong that you might not be able to appreciate during one season quite how different you can feel during others!

5

Understanding Your Mind

My 'mental' journey

"You think too much!" was often a criticism levelled at me in my late teens and early twenties in particular, which of course happened to coincide with one of the unhappiest periods of my life. To me, it certainly didn't appear random that I was having 'excessive thoughts' or overanalysing myself or my circumstances; it seemed to correlate. But a lot of people I met, who weren't aware of my individual qualities and sensitivities, probably couldn't make sense of the distress I was in. My life probably didn't appear to be particularly discordant to those around me. But it was for me.

I worked out that I seemed to *think* more when I was distressed. This hypothesis seemed pretty sound as I started to notice that when I was doing things that I liked, my mind was probably as airy, light and harmonious as the next person's. And actually given the amount of yoga and meditation I was doing – even back then – it was probably even lighter at times when the going was good!

But let's get one thing straight – we all think. It's a function of the mind that it creates thoughts, images and feelings based on our nervous system activity, so this idea that sometimes gets bandied around in the new age, particularly related to meditation, that you are somehow meant to magically have an empty mind, or that somehow you aren't successful as a meditator unless you have an empty mind, is a misconception.

However, there is a variance in the types, volume and 'density' of thoughts, and somewhere along the line I started to notice the relationship between my thoughts and the activities I was doing. I also began to notice that I appeared to have different 'thought themes' that would continually circle around in a pattern, rather than my mind just being random chaos.

Later, doing long or intense 'spiritual' practices such as Vipassana meditation, or Plant Spirit Medicine such as San Pedro, my awareness of thought patterns became even more apparent as I found myself developing an even stronger ability to 'witness' and observe my own mind.

Also doing so much meditation and similar practice, I began to become aware that 'I' am indeed a separate being than my mind – since if I could witness my mind, I'm obviously not it, if that makes some sense. (I actually think when we sit and witness our own mind we shift our perspective to soul consciousness, observing our personality self.)

Corresponding to my growing awareness of thought patterns were my studies on Taoism, yin and yang and the Five Elements. As I explained in the previous chapter, every facet of you can be placed in an elemental category – whether it's an organ, emotion or part of your musculoskeletal system.

I started to wonder, if an element shows so clearly on the exterior of the body and in your emotional animation when it's in a state of expression, then surely it must also show in your thoughts, in your 'inner' world too?

For example, the Fire Element is seen to correspond with your heart, small intestine, pericardium and triple heater, the emotion of joy, the sound of laughter, and our ability to animate and express. So it occurred to me that when my Fire Element is expressing itself, when I'm feeling joyful, laughing and so on, that must also correspond to the similar happy thoughts that are passing through my mind at the same time.

I started to watch my mind more closely and it became easier to identify and bracket certain types of thought and put them into Element categories and work out which organs were actually 'talking' to me. I would hear the obvious ones – like when I was *feeling* hungry I would also *think* 'I'm hungry' and thus be aware it was my stomach chatter (from my Earth Element) but then I started to identify the voice of my Wood Element (liver and gall bladder), Metal Element (lung and large intestine) and Water Element (kidney and bladder).

Before long, I started to get to know and respect the thoughts in my mind, and identify them as an expression of the organs giving me information. A vast amount of what passes through your mind is basically an extension of your body and nervous system talking to you, and deserves to be embraced and understood, just like any other part of your body.

This was a huge contrast to my early days of attempting to master, understand and work with the mind which would generally take one of two routes: trying to distract myself from it – TV, drink, activity and so on, or using 'spiritual' practices and things like meditation as a means of trying to circumvent, bypass, avoid or actually, in some ways, belittle the mind.

Having now developed a firmer understanding of what actually passes through my mind, I often reflect with a degree of annoyance on some of the early meditation teachings I attended, and likewise some workshops or events I come across even today. A great deal of these practices are concerned with either drilling home the constant need to 'let go' of what you are thinking, or in some respect belittling the mind. I attended one particular 'satsang' (a sitting with a spiritual teacher) where despite everyone being freely invited to share their questions, virtually every time anyone opened their mouths to share, the teacher appeared keen to tell them that it was 'just their mind talking' and to ignore it! So I can now see that while what I was trying to do in mastering the mind was admirable, it was also based a great deal on suppression and discomfort of my basic human instincts! This is often now referred to as 'spiritual bypassing'.

For me now, as I'll explain in the Nuts and Bolts Tutorial below, it's all about the discernment of what to listen to from within, and what to let drift on by. I feel those earlier experiences and teachings, directed at the wrong type of person (i.e. one who might already be confused or too passive in life, like I was) and the constant drilling to 'let it go' or that the mind is just spewing nonsense and to be 'ignored' or 'transcended' is actually not very helpful. It can just perpetuate even more strain and suppression, as the inner chatter you are hearing in your mind can actually be giving you fundamental information you need to move your life forward which will create more happiness and thus a quieter, stiller and more harmonious mind!

So get to know the beast, and start to understand it. I for one have found my life so much better and easier since I've done so!

I've transformed those early confused days to a point where I now run popular workshops on the mind where we actually map out thoughts and relate them to the corresponding organs. It's actually one of my favourites as it's such a passion for me, and because it's unique as it provides the mind 'map' combined with meditation techniques so we actually practise the self-observation. For people of a more Western mindset who like to understand concepts as well as experiential practices it can be particularly helpful, as never before have they seen the contents of their inner world mapped out so clearly!

Nuts and Bolts: Tutorial

Now we have looked at the manifestation of yin and yang and Five Elements in our outer experience, it's time to see how they appear in our inner world!

KEY POINT

The activity in your mind is linked to the activity in your nervous system - not just the amount of thoughts you are having, or their volume, but also the type of thoughts you are having.

So self-witnessing the mind allows you to see when the nervous system and thus mind is overstimulated, and by getting to know the characteristics of your internal dialogue you can actually work out which individual elements within you need particular attention.

Practices like yoga, meditation and deep relaxation and receiving treatments like acupuncture allow you to generate conscious control over the activity in the nervous system and therefore the mind!

The mind

Isn't it amazing that even with all the advances of modern medicine and the ability to register and record even the subtlest variances in our physical state that there is still so much confusion and so many differing perspectives on what the 'mind' is? And additionally, how various medical systems have such different perspectives on the extent of a body-mind connection at all.

For example, Chinese medicine sees an intimate connection between the body and mind whereas Western medicine identifies some links, but often takes what can be quite subtly nuanced mental states and puts them into quite broad categories such as 'depression', 'anxiety' and the many other labels we have nowadays for various mental conditions.

However, having such broad categorisations often doesn't do justice to the individual nature of these conditions for each person, whereas holistic systems enable us to identify with a greater degree of specificity the actual dynamics involved in each person's condition.

So, what is the mind?

This is a big question! And before I answer it I should mention that of course some people may have a very different experience of the mind than others, and some people may have an experience of the mind that is even beyond my comprehension and terms of reference.

However, putting what I don't know to one side and focusing on what I do, I can stand on fairly solid ground when I say that in the broadest sense your mind is a combination of both your internal and external senses.

So if you were able to observe and record the contents of your mind over a period of time, you would find that the contents would consist of the external senses of sight, sound, taste, touch and smell, alongside the senses of the signals that arise from 'within' the body.

For example, in one moment you might find yourself being conscious you are using your vision and seeing what's around you (external), then you might switch to an awareness you are hungry (internal), then switch to what you can hear around you (external), then find yourself reflecting on something that happened yesterday (internal), then become conscious of the odour in the room (external), then think about a loved one (internal) and so on!

This movement between the internal and external senses is the broader yin and yang pattern of the mind. And the cycling between the individual senses, both internal and external, can be seen as the expression of the Five Elements. So we can see that the mind also has readily identifiable patterns just like all other natural phenomena we explored in Chapter 4, and the mind is essentially just your own inner experience of the same patterns that pervade the natural world around you.

Image 5 illustrates the input from the external and internal senses and how they both become part of our 'mind' via the nervous system. The brain acts as a kind of processing station for all the signals.

MIND = Internal Senses + External Senses

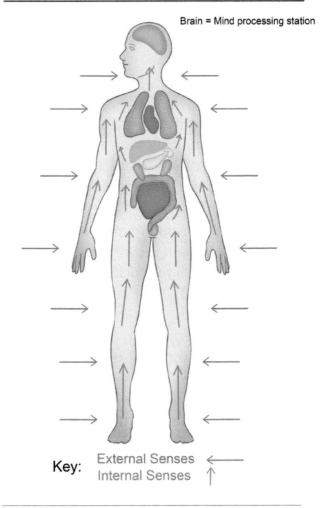

Brain = Mind processing station

Key:
External Senses ⟵
Internal Senses ↑

External Senses (5 Elements Without)		Internal Senses (5 Elements Within)
Sight	WOOD	Liver & Gall Bladder
Taste	FIRE	Heart & Small Intestine
Touch	EARTH	Spleen & Stomach
Smell	METAL	Lungs & Large Intestine
Sound	WATER	Kidney & Bladder

Image 5: What is the mind?
Copyright Richard Brook 2014

Observing your own mind

The idea that you can observe your own mind might appear a bit strange, particularly if you haven't done much meditation practice! But the premise is that since you're actually a soul and consciousness sitting within a body (a soul and consciousness which also exists independently of the body) and your conceptual thoughts are actually an extension of the functions of your body, you can also witness your own thoughts in exactly the same way you can witness any other part of your body!

Let's use the example of your leg. In some moments you have the ability to focus and observe your leg from the outside, to check out the feelings and sensations and watch it closely. At other times, you lose this observational capacity and the leg just becomes part of who you are, unconsciously. It's still there, but you aren't observing it. And sometimes the experience of your leg can overwhelm you – if it's in pain or discomfort sometimes it can obliterate virtually all other input.

It's also the same with your mind. You have phases of time where you can clearly witness and be aware of your own thoughts, and then other times where you just get lost in them and 'become' them. And similarly, when you are in mental pain and discomfort it can similarly overwhelm your perception.

Using the exercises in this section you can cultivate the ability to begin to self-observe much more keenly, to sit more fully in your soul and witness who you are. However, this is a brave and efficacious path, as sometimes we like to hang onto and identify with particular parts of our mind as being 'who we are', as an unconscious habit. And those particular parts of the mind also don't like the idea that they aren't actually running the show, so they will do anything to preserve their comfort zone. Perseverance is a good virtue here.

I am talking about meditation and mindfulness, and the ability, at will, to shift perspective to the vantage point of the soul. And don't worry if your mind sometimes still appears to be very busy – as we will explore in Chapter 7, it's a bit of a misconception that your mind has to be *still* to be in meditation as it's a process not a destination. Even though I've been practising many years, I sometimes still get lost in the myriad of thoughts that stream within. It's a continual process of refinement.

Going deeper: Observing yin and yang in the mind

KEY POINT

The mind follows the body, and the body follows nature

We identified in Chapter 4 that the body follows a natural pattern of yin and yang. As the mind is connected to the functions of the body, it therefore follows that the mind similarly follows this pattern.

This reflects in the mind having periods where it's naturally more focused outwards, in the external senses of sight, sound, taste, touch and smell, and periods of time where the mind is naturally more focused inwards, in the internal senses. Liken this dynamic to the seasonal polarity between summer, where the heat draws you out, and winter, where the cold draws you back in.

If you observe this movement between outer and inner, you can see that it happens in a general sense over the course of a day – during daylight hours you are more alert, and at night time you are more inward. For example first thing in the morning you may find that over 75% of the time your attention is more alert to the exterior senses, whereas last thing at night, you may find that 75% of the time you are drifting around within your own internal thoughts and senses with much less awareness to the outside. Obviously eventually you fall asleep where 100% of the time your mind is on the interior and the external senses are switched off.

However, you can be aware that this undulation between outer and inner actually happens in a much more micro sense too; there can be this fluctuation happening several times in one minute! You are alert, then drifting in your thoughts, then alert, and so on.

There are also ad hoc times during the day where yin or yang mind states naturally come to the fore in order to keep you balanced. If you have been very yang, outwardly focused and busy, the mind takes little opportunities when it can to head back inwards. You may find yourself 'taking a moment' where you can drift in reflection, sitting down with a cup of tea, 'collecting your thoughts', 'daydreaming' – where you are awake but your attention is inside. Or conversely, when too much of our attention has been sitting inside with too little stimulus, you get bored! So the mind seeks to head out and be engaged; you call a friend, walk out of the door, or watch a film.

KEY POINT

This movement of the mind between outer and inner is entirely natural and is linked to the functions of the body. To fight against it creates strain, imbalance and depletion within.

We often live in a 24/7 communication and stimulation culture which consistently strains our natural outward attention span – think for a moment of having a busy day and coming home to even more emails, texts, television on in the background, noisy neighbours, staring at a computer or phone screen (which irritates your nervous system) and bright street lighting when you are trying to unwind and go to sleep. Not forgetting the general stresses and strains you are carrying in your mind.

As we discussed in Chapter 4, the result of this overstimulation in the body is the yang organs become strained and the yin organs become depleted, and since in this case the mind is following the body, it's exactly the same. Your ability to stay focused becomes compromised, and the mind becomes restless! Remember your interior experience of the mind is a mirror for what's happening in the body generally.

There are a lot of misguided thoughts and beliefs around our ability to stay focused for extended periods of time (it's like some badge of honour as we take another caffeine pill to stay focused!). I'll repeat again, it's entirely natural for the mind to move inside and out and straining any one of these phases will mean the body-mind will naturally seek to move into the opposite phase to create balance.

A period of excessive focus, study, or work will strain you, so naturally you must let the mind rest afterwards and head in, otherwise you will become stressed.

This prevailing and unreasonable belief that you should be able to focus and concentrate excessively doesn't just permeate the world of work. During some of my early days of meditating I found that losing focus on the breath while meditating seemed to also come with an undercurrent of being frowned upon by various teachers!

Our ability to self-witness, however, is something which I would differentiate from focus or concentration. Self-witness is really where you have moved into the realm of the soul and it is possible to move into a state of profound witness where you can stay alert and still observe without strain, to various degrees, even when the mind moves inward. Indeed you are witnessing your entire being, your entire state, whether the mind is in or out. This is where we build insight – where we are observing our inner self!

We tend to have moments of self-witness (or 'self-realisation') as a matter of course, but it is also possible to maintain an extended phase of self-witness, particularly when the need to immerse or focus oneself in either the outer or inner mind is reduced. Sometimes our concentration on a certain outer or inner sense is so intense we can't help but become immersed in it – like when we are focusing on a task, or trying to 'figure something out'. However when I've had the need for this level of focus to be taken away, such as at a meditation retreat, then the alertness which would generally be spent focusing on specific tasks and the outer senses can be redirected inside and after several days of extensive practice it is possible to self-witness to a really profound degree.

Indeed, after several days of extensive meditation, since the body becomes rested from the practice, the need for the body to deeply rest and switch off to sleep also becomes less so you can even maintain awareness and self-witness during the night when you would normally have become 'unconscious' while sleeping.

However, the point remains that generally in everyday life, overstretching this natural undulation of the mind can create chronic imbalances in the organs, if it goes on for an excessive period of time, just like imbalanced physical activity can! All these imbalances, whether it's physical, mental, emotional or spiritual, affect the broader function of the organs as remember that in Chinese medicine the spectrum of an organ's function encompasses all these levels of your being!

Therefore how imbalances of yin and yang can manifest on the mental level is that you lose the clarity of being fully alert during the day, and fully switched off at night. So after a period of stress your organs might still be stuck in a pattern of overstimulation during the evening, thus creating a 'restless' state and difficulty sleeping, but then during the day, due to your organs not being sufficiently rested, you feel fatigued and drift off into your interior a lot as your yin seeks to resource. So you have moments where you appear 'vacant' as your organs seek to internally replenish and you withdraw from engaging with what's around you. This state can just continue to perpetuate, as it's difficult to recharge and rebalance if you can't rest properly. Of course this can also then become a repetitive cycle due to the body's circadian rhythm too. Therapeutic support at this point to balance the body-mind is very helpful!

Fusing yin and yang

As we will discuss further in Chapter 7, an associated benefit of directing your conscious awareness (yang) inwards to the messages from your body (yin) is you are actually creating a fusion of your own yin and yang (or left and right brain function, as I will explain later in the chapter) which in itself is a transformative, creative act which can bring balance. Think what happens when the yin and yang of humanity – men and women – are brought together; the strength of the interaction can be such that it can create new life!

For more on the fusion of yin and yang please visit this blog: Yin Yang of Awareness - Mind and Matter - The Alchemy of Creation[viii]

---

viii www.creativewellness.co.uk/bookblogs

Exercise: Observing the natural movement of yin and yang within the mind

Choose an external 'sensory anchor' to bring your awareness to. I often recommend using touch – for example the clothing resting on your abdomen just below the belly button (or the sensation of the flesh in that position itself), or you can also try using an external sound to focus on, or even a few minutes of each.

Ultimately you could actually use any external sense: the odour in the room, the taste in your mouth, or even sight, but for now, try touch and sound.

This external sensory awareness we relate to as being a 'yang' focus. So, by choosing an external sensory anchor to focus your awareness, you can then become aware of when the mind naturally transitions from this yang focus and pulls you back 'inside' into a yin orientation. When the mind transitions to a yin state you experience your inner thoughts, or a drifting within your thoughts and feelings with little or no external awareness.

Observe how the mind moves between these inner and outer states. Sometimes the mind moves rapidly between them; you can focus on the abdomen and then a moment later be lost in thought, then back to your abdomen, or sometimes much more slowly, particularly when the nervous system slows down.

Sit in self-observation for 10 minutes (you could try seven minutes using touch as an anchor, three minutes using sound) which should be long enough to notice this natural pattern.

Repeat this exercise daily for one week, both in the

morning and evening, to gain self-awareness of how your mind naturally moves between the interior and exterior and also how both your levels of alertness in these states can change at different times of day. Often in the morning we can have a much clearer external awareness, whereas at night we spend more time 'inside'.

Going deeper: Observing the five elements of the mind - the internal senses

We've identified that the mind moves to the 'interior' and we hear the 'internal senses' talking to us. Essentially those internal senses are the resonance of the organs and elements within our body 'talking' to us.

Here we'll look in detail at the associated thoughts and feelings we experience for the organs and elements and get to know them. This also enables us to take things a stage further and begin to discern when we may have a general imbalance in that element, or whether the imbalance is created by circumstances around us that are distressing the element.

Before moving on to explore the inner voices of the Five Elements, and how to distinguish them, first we need to get a fuller understanding of how those inner voices we hear in our mind are initially created.

The process of learning language from conception

When we are first born and within our early stages of development, what we experience within our mind is just direct sensory input both from the world around us – the five external senses of sight, sound, taste, touch and smell as identified earlier – and also simply the sensation and resonance of the inner organs, the five internal elements as we are exploring them now.

This means we would directly experience both the outer and inner senses without any accompanying conceptual narrative or 'inner dialogue' as the language centre of the mind at this stage has yet to be developed.

On a rudimentary level, a way to identify these functions of instinct and language would be to use the model of right brain and left brain function. We can associate the direct feeling from what we experience on the sensory level as being 'right brain' function, whereas the ability to create concepts in the mind develops later as 'left brain' function.

Learning language related to the 'internal' senses

For example, in your very early development when you would feel hungry, you would just *feel* hungry, the sensations of desiring food originating from the stomach and spleen (Earth Element), but you would not have the mental level conceptual language of 'I am hungry' to accompany the feeling. Basically, you didn't yet have the capacity to create the language in your mind – nor had you been taught it – to associate with the feeling.

So, as we continue to grow from our early days, we are then taught that the words 'I am hungry' are representative of that feeling of hunger. And as the left brain language centre of the mind continues to develop then it begins to accompany the feeling of hunger with the words 'I am hungry!' that you have learned. As we fully evolve we start to experience both the right side of the brain feeling the experience of being hungry, and the left side giving the language we associate with that feeling.

Learning language related to the 'external' senses

The process of experiencing and learning language around external sensory input of sight, sound, taste, touch and smell is exactly the same. For example, let's say that your parents are leaning over the side of your crib looking at you as the precious child that you are, radiating their love for you, and you are feeling that.

What you would be experiencing would be the tangible radiance and warmth of their open-heart energy enveloping you (if you want to get scientific it would be their electromagnetic field) and feeling beautiful subtle sensations as it interacts with your body. However, without the development of the language centre, the experience would simply be the sensations and feelings but without a conceptual language dialogue in your mind, as you haven't yet learned any language to accompany the feeling.

And then obviously later, once we develop the language centre, we would experience the feeling and then also think things like, 'Wow that feels nice', or 'I feel loved', and we then would apply that language to the feeling.

Or to look at a more pronounced, more physical, example, you could imagine a part from a toy has somehow made its way into your crib and you are lying on it and it is irritating your shoulder. Again, you would just feel the sense of irritation, but later on when the language centre has developed the same feeling may then come with the inner dialogue in mind of 'Ouch, that hurts' and so on.

Overthinker?

If you feel you are the type of person who 'overthinks' or overidentifies with your thoughts, just reflect for a moment that there was a time in your life where all you experienced was simply direct sensory input and direct instinctive expression, without any conceptual level thoughts at all!

And just think, that simple instinctive awareness of what you need, and what you need to express, is still within you now so it's really good to remember this if you feel you are being complicated in your mind!

KEY POINT

The fundamental point is that the language we experience in the mind is built upon both the internal and external sensory inputs that we are having. And fundamentally, this is still the same even as an evolved adult.

By identifying this link between sensory input and the amount and kind of inner dialogue, we have the opportunity to understand and manage to some degree the inner chatter by managing the sensory inputs.

Some of this is really obvious. For example if someone is playing blaring loud music that isn't to your taste it is annoying your external senses, so you have lots of internal chatter of 'I hate this music' and thus you ask them to turn it down. Problem solved. Or over a long period every time you walk into your work you notice that your body contracts and you get lots of internal chatter of 'I hate this job' and then you start to think about getting a new job.

But what if the sources of the internal chatter in your mind aren't so obvious? What if in fact it becomes virtually impossible to track what might be creating the trains of thought as it bears little resemblance to what is going on in your life? What about if you are walking around with a constant confused internal chatter virtually no matter what you are doing, and it follows you around everywhere?

The chances are that some of your internal physiology is imbalanced and stressed and as a result constantly creating internal dialogue as a sign that you need help – which is where of course natural therapies come into play, which we will look at in greater detail in Chapter 7.

KEY POINT

The trick is in working out whether the distress is coming from inside or outside! We need to manage and optimise both things: the external input that we choose to engage with in our lives, and also the internal senses we experience inside.

If the internal physiology and organs are imbalanced, they will constantly create troubled internal dialogue which we then project out onto whatever situation is in front of us, whether it's our work, our personal life or home life, etc. And the temptation then is that we start to change the circumstances around us, trying to 'fix it' when it's actually our imbalanced perception that is the problem, so it might not always be in our best interest to change what's going on around us.

So we need to learn to get to know our inner self, the inner voices of the elements, so we can work out what we tend to chronically generate and project onto the world around us, and also start to bring it back to balance using therapies and natural healing practices.

When we are more familiar with our inner selves in this way, we can be clearer and more confident when it is actually genuinely something from outside of us that is bothering us.

Understanding the Five Elements' voices within

Image 6 shows how the organs themselves impact and shape what we think, creating the running commentary and projections which often overlay our daily tasks and activities.

Reminder: When I refer to organs, it's within the context that the organ is connecting to a broader spectrum of intelligence that encompasses, and operates via, a meridian system and connects to physical, mental, emotional and spiritual faculties as well as a corresponding aspect of your soul – a much broader range of capacities than just the physical structure of the organ itself (see Chapter 4).

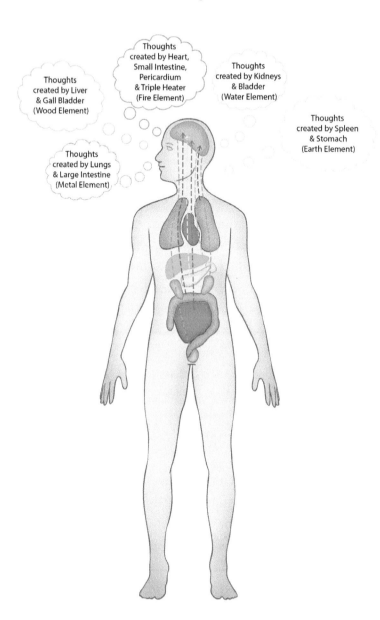

Image 6: The connection between organs and thought
Copyright Richard Brook 2019

Observing the Five Elements within the mind

"What is essential is invisible to the eye."
Antoine de Saint-Exupéry

Sometimes when observing your own mind you will be able to stay acutely aware of a great deal of the internal chatter in the moment as it's actually happening, but sometimes when the mind fluctuates to a very 'yin' and deep internal state you lose awareness of the thoughts you are experiencing – much like when you are asleep – but as the mind naturally swings back to the exterior quite quickly you can then quickly reflect and make a mental note of what you just experienced in the mind while you weren't consciously aware.

This is similar to how when you wake from a dream, as the more alert and conscious mind switches back on, you can make a mental note of what you were dreaming about. Remember, this undulation between being deep on the interior ('lost in thought' as we commonly call it) and being alert can also happen several times even across the course of a couple of minutes.

It's best not to get too complicated about this self-awareness (mindfulness) we are beginning to cultivate. In essence it's just the same as when someone asks you, "What are you thinking about?" and you catch yourself and become aware of your own thoughts and relay them. In this case, though, you have to do the 'catching' without the prompting of others!

It is particularly beneficial to train our awareness by doing dedicated observation (mindfulness) exercises, where we set aside a few minutes to closely observe the mind. This can help us to begin to become aware of aspects of our mind that otherwise we just tend to space out into, get lost in, or simply think it's 'who we are'. We often have one particular inner voice that we relate to as being 'who we are' when in essence all the voices of the elements are an aspect of us.

So, having a dedicated self-observation technique for a dedicated period of time keeps drawing you out of identifying with the inner chatter and 'becoming it' and challenges you to observe it – to stay in the vantage point of the soul observing the mind.

Image 7 shows a broad description of the various inner voices that correspond to each element within you.

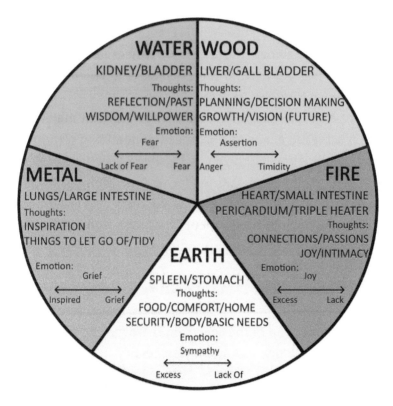

Image 7: The Five Elements of your mind

The spectrum of the internal dialogue and emotion

In a similar way to how the characteristics of the external elements can present across a spectrum, depending on their balance (e.g. someone could have lots of red or lack of red, laugh excessively or barely at all), so it's also the same with how we experience the characteristics of the elements internally.

Table 4 gives an indication of the range of internal dialogue associated with each element in greater detail.

When the elements express they may have a distinct emotional feeling accompanying the dialogue if the corresponding organs are particularly strongly activated in you. If you don't get a discernible emotional feeling alongside the thoughts it's fine – the organs are either relatively at peace or you've just got used to their default emotional resonance as the norm for how you feel.

For example, the voice of the Wood Element may sound like a sergeant major in your head announcing clear, rigid plans, or it may sound like a balanced visionary that has a plan of how to get you where you are going, or it may sound like a timid voice, lacking decision and vision. And emotionally, while the element is strongly activated within you, you may feel a corresponding sense of anger, positive assertion or timidity.

Or while the Fire Element is active you may have lots of loving or passionate thoughts and feel a warm sense of joy or at the other end of the spectrum there may be thoughts of despondency, loneliness and joylessness.

Table 4: The presentation of the elements within the mind

Element	Organs	Spectrum of internal voice (internal dialogue)		
		Element in excess	Balanced	Element deficient
Wood	Liver / Gall bladder	Sergeant major type thoughts, clear vision, rigid instructions, excessive planning and decision making.	'Happy wanderer'; you have a plan so you know where you are going, but also some flexibility.	Timid, uncertain thoughts related to vision or direction, feeling deficient in asserting self, confusion around plans and decisions.
Fire	Heart, small intestine / Pericardium, triple heater	Predominance of thoughts around passions in life, sexual and intimate thoughts, strong desire for intimate connection, excitement and creating fun. Thoughts about wanting to be the centre of attention.	Passionate and warm thoughts without feeling overbearing, sense of discernment around relationships and ability to sense and hear others.	Despondency, dispassionate, thoughts of feeling 'locked in' and trapped in expressing connection (either giving or receiving), feeling nothing turns you on (in all areas of life).
Earth	Spleen / Stomach	Thoughts of robust confidence in self, desire to nourish and nurture self and others to excess, thoughts about collecting an abundance of resources.	Thoughts of contentment, being aware of what you need to fulfil basic needs and thoughts of feeling satisfied and comfortable in your body.	Worrying about basic needs, feeling insecure, lacking sympathy, feeling unsatisfied, lack of desire to nourish self or others.
Metal	Lung / Large intestine	Lots of amazing ideas (that seem to float through without output), focus on clarity, cleanliness and structure.	Feeling well organised and structured, fresh, able to integrate new ideas and let go of old.	Trouble letting go, grief stricken, feeling cluttered with old thoughts and feelings, struggling to grasp structure or concepts.
Water	Kidney / Bladder	Extreme inner drive and determination to get things done, in a rush, feeling reckless and fearless and not concerned with lessons learned from the past.	Conscious of ability to manage energy reserves and actions appropriately. Sense of wisdom after reflecting on past.	Lack of willpower, uncertainty of inner reserves, fearful, lots of introspection and reflection but little action.

For more on the internal voices you hear in your mind, please visit these blogs (the first blog also contains an example of the subsequent exercise detailed below): Understanding How the Mind Works[ix] and The Five Elements of your mind[x]

Why is it important to be aware of our inner dialogue?

The more we start to observe our inner dialogue the sharper our awareness becomes, and then of course we can start to become more and more aware of the origin, nature and themes of our thoughts and their messages and intelligence. In many respects this exercise of self-awareness is about bringing our conscious awareness to what are often seen as the subconscious voices in our mind.

By getting to know your inner voices, and the general internal calibration of your organs, you can make life a lot easier and also be aware of what an internally generated imbalance is rather than an external one, and act accordingly.

This dynamic of knowing whether 'it's us' or 'the situation' which is the source of our distress in life is massive in terms of what it means for our personal growth. Not being able to discern the difference is the internal equivalent of blaming the road for your rough ride, when it's the suspension of the car that is actually damaged. Or going for a run if you have a bad knee, and then thinking that running per se is a debilitating thing to do – once the knee is healed, you know you will be stronger and enjoy it more!

---

ix   www.creativewellness.co.uk/bookblogs
x   www.creativewellness.co.uk/bookblogs

Many people who have never looked inside and don't understand their own constitutional balance tend to solely blame external circumstances or try to get everything around them to mould to their desire and state, as they are looking from a vantage point of believing that they are a 'fixed' entity who has no scope for change.

Once you start to appreciate that in fact you also have internal limitations and the scope for change – as far as nature will allow – this can enable you to appreciate that sometimes the imbalance that lies within us is also partly contributing to making life difficult. Sometimes it's both ends of the spectrum that need work – we need to fine-tune what we choose to engage with, and work on ourselves too, which we'll be exploring techniques for in Chapter 7.

I emphasise we have scope for change 'as far as nature will allow' as we don't want to get into a situation where we always actually 'blame' ourselves either for any perceived weaknesses or difficulties we have. This is at the opposite end of the spectrum to those who tend to blame everything around them, and I've also met plenty of people who actually blame their own internal state for everything. This is also futile and missing the point.

The essence of what I'm trying to teach is appreciating and knowing who you are, which includes accepting your unique qualities and working to improve what you can. And then by knowing who you are, you can work out more clearly when something outside of you just doesn't suit you, without blame or judgement. It's essential to keep your inner state finely tuned and maintained, so that you know your perception is accurate, and you enjoy and feel proud of the individuality of who you are!

Exercise: Observing the Five Elements within the mind

The process for this exercise is similar to the observation of the yin and yang patterns of the mind exercise earlier in this chapter, where we track the natural movement of the mind between inner and outer, except in this exercise you also track the specific nature of your thoughts while the mind has moved to the interior and is producing internal dialogue.

Choose an external 'sensory anchor' to bring your awareness to. Again, we'll use touch – the sensation of your clothing resting on your abdomen just below the belly button (or the sensation of the flesh in that position itself).

This external sensory awareness we relate to as being a yang focus. So by choosing an external sensory anchor to focus your awareness on you can then become aware of when the mind naturally transitions from this yang focus and pulls you back 'inside' into a yin orientation. When the mind transitions to a yin state you experience your inner thoughts, or a drifting within your thoughts and feelings with little or no external awareness.

However, in this exercise track the specific nature of your thoughts while the mind has moved to the interior and is producing internal dialogue. You can often become aware of what you have been thinking about when the mind moves naturally back to an external focus.

It's essential that the attention and focus is diligently placed back on the external sensory anchor of touch or flesh beneath the belly button as it's this focus on the exterior which then creates the polarity (or rebound) for the mind to head back 'inside' again. Without the focus you essentially just drift in thought with much less distinction between internal and external states.

After the exercise make a written note of the actual themes and dialogue you heard in your mind and which elemental category they fall into.

Sit in self-observation for at least 10 minutes which should be long enough for you to begin to notice naturally occurring patterns. Try and build up to 20 minutes within a few days - the longer you sit for, the more the nervous system relaxes, and it's easier for the mind to head 'inside' so you can observe it.

Repeat this exercise daily for one week. Try moving the time around so you can see that you tend to think of different things at different times of day (as different elements are more prominent at different times of the day).

Identifying the voices within

As your inner awareness increases you may be able to start to pick up discernible patterns of your inner voices, and which ones are most prominent.

You can of course also marry together your acute awareness generated through the exercises with your awareness of how you normally think throughout your life, as it will likely be a more detailed version of your existing thought patterns. We can, however, in our day-to-day life, choose to 'tune out' certain inner voices, so the exercises make sure you observe all of them!

However, don't be too quick to draw conclusions about the default, inherent state of the elements based on initial exercises as remember, the efficacy of the exercise is built up over time in that by getting to know your organs and internal voices you can begin to work out whether they are stressed, or happy and thriving – and how your life choices can also be affecting this.

So really, you need to carry this self-awareness of your internal dialogue through a few different situations in your life so you can work out the more 'default' setting of your elements as opposed to ones that are acutely created by your present life circumstances. Then of course if we can work out that it is acute situations that are upsetting our balance, we can start doing something about them.

Let's look at some specific examples of what you may be experiencing in your inner world.

Water Element

Reminder: The kidney and bladder comprise the Water Element and come with an associated internal voice on a spectrum related to reflection, wisdom, willpower and with an emotional correspondence on the spectrum of fear.

For example, if you do the exercise (or even just when you become inwardly aware at other times) and you hear a strong 'fear' or 'excessive caution' narrative in your mind it could mean a couple of things.

Firstly, if this inner voice of fear is a constant voice for you, then it could mean you have an inherent imbalance in your kidney and bladder organs which means they aren't quite feeding you with the resources or sense of strength to move out into the world that you are capable of.

This could be from a constitutional deficiency that could be treated and supported through acupuncture or other therapies, yoga or deep relaxation, or indeed other therapeutic lifestyle changes.

In essence, if no matter what you do, even if the circumstances around you are good you are still hearing that voice of fear, then it would indicate this kind of constitutional imbalance. This conclusion would also be supported if you are aware that you have had that fear or excessive caution voice for as long as you can remember, and it has come with you through many situations in your life. Evidently, like all other imbalances, this kind of imbalance can hold you back in life.

Or, secondly, it could be that you may just be hearing this voice at this time because of imbalances relating to your present life circumstances, which are stressing those organs and thus this element within you.

On a practical level, this could be because you aren't getting enough rest, drinking enough water or simply not going with your flow. Since your kidney and bladder are full of fluid, which becomes imprinted with your unique vibration, they have an inherent sense of where they wish to flow – just as when you pour a glass of water on the floor the water will find its path of least resistance so you have an inherent instinct of what similarly flows in your life.

If you aren't going with your flow then essentially it creates stress on the organs, a bit like trying to push water in directions it doesn't want to go – apart from creating stress it will also deplete your energy away from the things that you really instinctively do want to do.

But while recognising that this may be an acute imbalance related to your present life circumstances, you need to observe the inner voice of your Water Element over a period of time, so you can have perspective to ascertain there has been a change.

For example, if you reflect back and are conscious that you didn't have that fear voice a few months ago when perhaps you had a different job, or it goes away when you consider changing direction in life, or when you drink more water or get more rest, then it's a sign it could well be an acute imbalance as it's relatively changeable depending on circumstances.

Wood Element

Reminder: The liver and gall bladder comprise the Wood Element and come with an associated internal voice related to planning and decision making, having vision and being able to assert yourself, with an emotional correspondence on the spectrum of assertion.

For example, if you do the exercise (or even just when you become inwardly aware at other times) and you hear a pronounced and rigid planning and decision-making narrative in your mind, and feel a sense of anger or frustration, it could mean a couple of things.

If you recognise over time this tends to be a relatively constant inner experience for you, it could indicate that the chronic inherent state of your Wood Element is one of excess and it could benefit from treatment to fine-tune it somewhat.

Or if you recognise that it only appears at this particular time, and that usually that part of you is more relaxed, then again it could be an indication that the Wood Element is responding to some present acute circumstances in your life – and indicating the desire for change or adjustment.

It could be that you are coming off track from your instinctive vision for what you need to thrive, so the organs are becoming agitated and trying to create or push a new plan all the time to get you back on track, or it could relate to more practical matters such as that you are eating a diet too rich in fat that is stressing the organs, drinking too much alcohol or you aren't physically moving enough or expressing yourself fully, all of which also stress the organs.

Observing this voice over time, you can start to get an indication of what the organs' default states are, and then when they're flaring up and giving you information!

Fire Element

Reminder: The heart, small intestine, pericardium and triple heater comprise the Fire Element and come with an associated internal voice around relationships, connection and passion, with a corresponding emotional spectrum around joy.

So, for example, if you get to know your Fire Element, and notice that no matter how much intimacy, close relationships, and occupations and activities you participate in that none really bring you joy, you never feel that relationships touch you deeply and your internal chatter always says is that it's never enough, then you could have an inherent imbalance in your Fire Element. So of course, rather than constantly blaming the external circumstance and moving from relationship to relationship, having some internal therapy on your Fire Element could be the way forward.

Or conversely, if you are aware that your internal Fire Element generally ticks over nicely, feeling joyful and passionate in life and relationships, but you begin to experience feelings of joylessness in a relationship or lack of passion, then it helps you to ascertain that it could be externally generated by the circumstances.

Earth Element

Reminder: The stomach and spleen comprise your Earth Element and the inner voice operates on a spectrum related to comfort, nourishment and security, and comes with an emotional correspondence on the spectrum of sympathy.

So, for example, if you hear a voice of lack of satisfaction, worry or inability to process things that have happened and you also recognise that over time this tends to be the default inner experience of that voice, it could indicate that the chronic inherent state of your Earth Element is out of balance and it could benefit from treatment.

Or if you recognise that it only appears at this acute time, and that usually you feel satisfied, it could be an indication that the Earth Element is responding to some present acute circumstances in your life. This could be something quite practical and physical: that you haven't been eating food that nourishes you, or it could be an indication that the things you are choosing to spend your time on aren't working for you, or that you don't feel happy with your nest, where you are choosing to live.

Metal Element

Reminder: The lungs and large intestine comprise your Metal Element and come with an associated inner voice on a spectrum relating to inspiration and letting go (what to keep and what to throw away) as well as an emotional correspondence on the spectrum of grief.

So, for example, if you hear a voice of lack of inspiration and thinking that things were always better in the past, and pining for the past and feeling grief for what has been lost, and you also recognise that over time this tends to be the default inner experience of that voice, it could indicate that the chronic inherent state of your Metal Element is out of balance and it could benefit from treatment.

Or if you recognise that it only appears at this acute time, and that usually you feel quite inspired and don't hold onto the past, then it could be an indication that the Metal Element is responding to some present acute circumstances in your life. This could be something quite practical and physical: that your large intestine has become bogged down with toxicity or the lungs aren't being opened with exercise or you aren't engaging with the things that inspire you.

Coming full circle - the entire spectrum of Five Elements in your life

Image 8 shows the full spectrum of the elemental correspondences all the way through from our inner world to how they can be seen to present in our outer world. So remember an imbalance in any aspect – either on inner manifestation of the elements or outer – can negatively affect you, as all layers of your being, including your outer world, interact.

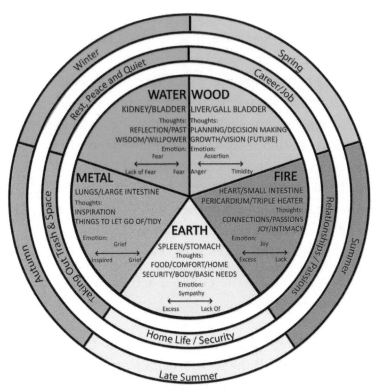

Image 8: The interplay between seasons, areas of your life, organs, thoughts and emotions

Copyright Richard Brook 2014

Internal conflict and arguments

In an ideal situation, each element is getting what it needs from your life around you and is happy so the internal elements are in concert within you – your internal voices are at peace. Remember it's built into you as a natural being to reach out for what you need to balance, so following your instincts is key.

However, sometimes you may notice that your internal elements actually argue with one another. In fact sometimes when we are really out of balance it can seem like a mass brawl going on inside your mind.

It's not unusual to have a single issue going on in your life that each internal element within you seems to hold a different opinion on. I remember observing this in my own mind once when a relationship was coming to an end. In quick-fire fashion each element seemed to offer its opinion. My Fire was saying, "Oh but you love her," my Wood was saying, "It's just time to move on" and creating a vision for the 'next' person, my Earth was saying, "Oh but she's such a lovely girl," throwing in the sympathy, my Metal was saying, "It's time to let go, it's just finished," and my Water was saying, "This just doesn't flow any more!"

Who is in overall control?

So when you have internal conflict going on, it's a good time to do your practices such as yoga and meditation alongside activities that bring you into your body and heart (as you identified in the exercises in chapter 2) so you can access the overarching voice of the soul which gives direction through the heart. Ultimately, coming back to what we learned in that chapter, the heart is in overall command, and if this state appears to be slipping away, then you need to do your heartfelt practices to re-establish balance.

And please note, don't mistake the idea of your heart being in control as necessarily meaning you are always making somewhat 'affectionate' decisions. In this context, the heart knows what is best for you – which includes saying no and moving on!

Because the heart connects to the vantage point of the

soul, from there you can then also start to witness the broader perspective of both your life and your internal elements. You can sometimes witness your internal elements almost like distressed children who have been operating without enough parental guidance, but since you are then activating your heart, it helps to call the elements back into alignment.

And when the heart is in control the elements are working in alignment to keep you balanced. By each playing out their individual role within the soul's bigger plan:

- Your Wood Element provides the vision, plans and asserts the decisions
- Your Fire Element provides the passions and intimate relationships to fulfil
- Your Earth Element provides the raw resources and comfort
- Your Metal Element provides the inspiration and gets rid of what you no longer need
- Your Water Element provides the wisdom and willpower to get things done

For example, if your Water Element has that constitutional tendency to a voice of fear – even if you look after it in your lifestyle – then when you make a change it might start to kick up like a small child and make a protest!

But if you are content that the overall flow and direction you are heading in is the way of the soul then you can see this inner voice as a child with you as the parent, and sometimes you just need to hold its hand and take it with you wherever you are going! The voice may not ever change, but it will stop holding you back in life.

How your balance of 'left' and 'right' brain function can affect your inner experience

While our inner experience is made up of the signals from the organs and then our mind creating language from those signals, each person's individual left brain and right brain balance can create some variance as to how they experience these faculties. This is because, as I discussed earlier, in a rudimentary sense the left brain relates more to the conceptual and language aspects of the mind, whereas the right brain is more connected to the feelings and emotions.

Therefore more right brain oriented people may find their inner experience is one of being more conscious of feelings and emotions, whereas more left brain people may find a greater experience in their mind of language, and to a lesser extent the experience of the feelings themselves. So the ratio in your inner experience of language as compared to feelings can be different.

Therefore if you are more right brain oriented, you may find it easier to connect to the direct emotional resonance of each of the elements, such as happy, sad, angry, frustrated, strong, fearful, etc. By contrast left brain people will relate more to the conceptual language that associates with the feeling: "I am feeling happy, sad, etc".

It is a worthwhile exercise to see how well you can both feel the feelings, and also articulate them as words. Left brain oriented people may struggle with really accessing the sensations and textures of how they feel, but can explain in words how they feel, whereas right brain oriented people may find it easier to feel the feelings and more difficult to articulate them in language.

This can also reflect in how people instinctively like to *process* their feelings. Left brain people might find it easier to write and talk, and right brain people might find themselves more drawn to creating art as an expression. Whatever you normally do, it can be healthy to try the opposite to create balance! If you are very left brain it can be good to get more into your body – use dance and movement as a means of expressing and experiencing your feelings. If you are right brain oriented, try writing down or explaining to someone how you feel.

The ego - friend or foe?

Ego. How often does that word come up, especially in new age and personal development circles? People also often like to bring up the subject of 'ego' when it suits them to pass judgement on other people's behaviour while on some complicated new age trip about how you should be living and relating to the mind.

But does anyone really clearly know what people are talking about when they mention ego?

Since the mind is full of various voices, some of direct intelligence from the organs within, then how are we meant to know which ones are the mythical ego? Is it ego when your Earth Element is telling you that you are hungry? Is it ego when your Wood Element creates a vision in your mind to try and get a certain job because instinctively you know it's for your best potential? One person's 'ego' could be another person's destiny! It's subjective, so how do we know?

Well, my take on it is that ego can be seen as any inner voice which betrays the desire of the soul, as your soul is attuned to the great universal intelligence which gives you direction for the greater good in your life. So the soul is trying to give you authentic prompts and expressions of your greater good, whereas ego tends to consist of mental level projections and ideas that hold you back – based on past experiences.

In essence, the ego can't see the infinite possibilities that the soul is attuned to, because it's working from the back catalogue of things that have happened previously, so it only has a limited set of references, whereas in reality there are an endless stream of fresh possibilities occurring in any one moment. Where 'ego' really kicks in is where it starts to significantly impinge upon the healthy expression of our soul.

Let's look at some basic examples of how this can develop. Firstly, let's look at one of the more common perspectives of what we consider 'ego' to be, where it is associated with a disproportionate sense of self-worth.

Let's take the example of a young child, who when they express an interest in taking up a new activity, are repeatedly told that they are wonderful, that they are more important than anyone else around them, and just to do what they want and not care how their actions affect others. Over time the vibration of this communication is absorbed into the body, and starts to become part of the person's inner dialogue associated with making choices.

So, let's fast forward 20 years and when the soul is giving a prompting for the person to move forward in an area of their life, it may be accompanied with an 'ego' voice that only they are important and no one else matters. So, in this case, the old, discordant, selfish thought can supersede their innate soul level awareness of others.

However, we also identify the same process of suggestive language being absorbed and how it creates a 'negative' ego voice and lack of self-worth. For example, let's say a child was repeatedly told, when they expressed they were hungry, "No you're not, you can go without." What happens is the vibration of that communication gradually gets absorbed into the body-mind. Over time, it begins to interfere with the highest functioning of the body-mind potential, as alongside feeling hungry, the person also now experiences the inner dialogue of, "No you're not, you can go without!"

In this case the internal expression associated with the Earth Element of the spleen and stomach – which indicates when we are hungry – has become tainted with the 'ego' voice of not being worthy to eat and starts to supersede their own delicate self-care and prompting of the soul.

It can also depend which organs or element has been 'injured' and affected' by the previous experiences as to the nature of the ego voice we will experience. If the kidneys were particularly out of balance, a person may have a pronounced 'fear' or 'lack of fear' ego; if it was the liver, a person may have a pronounced 'anger' or 'timidity' ego, and so on. The organs are actually trying to give us an accurate appraisal of the situation but are affected by previous experiences.

We are all prey to the vagaries of the ego in one way or another as it lurks and taints our thoughts at every corner, but the degree to which it takes hold of you depends on how connected to your heart you are. Since the heart houses the soul, and the soul connects to the aforementioned universal intelligence, when you are attuned to the heart you are attuned to the greater needs of the universe itself, the universal 'One'.

And how you begin to transcend ego over time is by

doing as many things as possible and spending as much time as possible with the heart and soul at the forefront of your life. Then the blood passing through your heart gets stamped with the soul level intelligence, so you physically become, and begin to radiate the intelligence of the soul through your body, replacing the old discordant patterns.

The discordant patterns and energies start to break down as when the soul sits fully in the body the vibration is so high it starts to disperse old heavy, discordant thought-forms (which actually become the ego patterns), which get in the way of us being a true channel of universal intelligence. So again, it's essential you have activities and occupations in your life where you engage with your individual soulful expression, or therapeutic modalities where you similarly access soul intelligence.

However, some patterns can be very heavily ingrained, and it's good to become aware of them. A sign of a heavily ingrained pattern can be if you keep getting a repetitive thought form or memory which you keep projecting onto your life.

Just remember that the future is unwritten and the subtle nuances of what you may experience are sometimes beyond the comprehension of the conceptual mind so it produces clunky old thought forms and memories to fill the void and try and keep you on safe territory. Try again to access the subtle intelligence of the heart around these matters, rather than the back catalogue of the mind and projections.

Alongside the techniques we discussed in Chapter 2 around accessing and embodying the soul, we'll also look at some practices which quieten and balance the mind in Chapter 7 so you can tune back into the intelligence of your heart and soul in order to be guided from there more fully.

Where your inner dialogue has its limitations - the role of instinct

While getting to know the voice of your organs is essential and extremely beneficial, it's also essential to not lose touch with your instincts, and your respect and understanding of them. We can also sometimes lose connection to our instincts if we spend too much time focusing on the dialogue we are hearing in our mind, and inhibiting, suppressing or overanalysing our instinctive reactions.

It's obviously fine to maintain a strong awareness of your inner dialogue when you are sitting and reflecting or doing a meditation exercise as there is very little outer stimulus and you have created the circumstances in order to be able to go 'inside'. But in real time interaction, the key point is that your instincts actually move more quickly than your thoughts can!

So while we want to keep some awareness of the whispers of our soul, sometimes we don't have time to think in a calculated way and we have to rely on our heart and instincts as our navigational tools to guide us. Remember your heart is the instrument of the soul so equally trust its intelligence and instinctive guidance to what you are interacting with in the present moment, just in the same way you can trust the actual whispers of your soul when the mind is quietened enough to hear it!

It's just as magnificent to marvel at and witness your instinctive responses to something and then have introspection and sort your thoughts afterwards when the mind pulls you back inside. Even if you are sitting in deep meditation and someone suddenly shouts and throws a ball to you, you're not really going to have a chance to listen to all the various conversations from your internal organs before having to stick an arm out and catch it!

So while we like to listen to the 'good stuff' in the mind, getting lost in the endless other stories isn't such a good idea, as alongside the useful 'in the moment' direct intelligence of the elements and soul talking to you, it also just tends to play out reflections from the past or projections for the future (which are based on reflections from the past!). It's a bit like the mind is doing laundry and trying to wash through all it's already experienced. Investing in these thoughts is a bit like investing in the dirty water after you have already washed your clothes in it – not so useful!

Preconceptions: Who we 'think' we are versus who we really are

We also have to be very careful about who we *think* we are. This is because what we often do is start to align our identity with the stories that play in our mind (as they can sometimes appear as quite a significant part of our make-up) when in reality we are so much more than that.

In any one moment your experience is made up of the cumulative input of emotions and vibrations from all organs in the body as well as the sensory input from the environment around you. In addition to this there are the expressive instincts from your spontaneous self, *as well as* the mental level stories playing in your mind. Be very careful these mental level stories don't start to drown the other levels out, as sometimes the stories become like old friends and we seek solace in their company!

It's essential to remember the stories which play in your

mind are not your spontaneous self in the moment, and as discussed earlier the body and nervous system responds to situations and events way quicker than your mental level channel can change its story. Indeed, the mind often continues playing a similar story no matter what is actually going on around us!

Revisiting the vibration and music analogy from Chapter 3, we want to make sure we are really moving and feeling the vibrations of what is really going on around us. If we become too 'thick skinned' and dense we lose our ability to spontaneously and instinctively react and move with what we engage with.

Therefore we'll explore in Chapter 7 techniques to keep our energy body clear and sharpen our instincts so we can make sure we stay truly attuned to what's going on around us, and truly engage with life.

Forget what's happening in the commentary box and keep your eyes on what is actually happening on the pitch!
Richard Brook, 1999

Let's go a little bit deeper with how easily we can fall into this pattern of preconception. This is an example that we've probably all experienced at times, of when we are hungry but don't know in our 'mind' what we want. This is because the mind can't sometimes come up with an image subtle and individual enough to meet the exact requirements of the signals that your body is feeding back to you in the moment, so you simply play 'old meals' through the mind, from the previous memories of what you've eaten, and can end up making a choice based on that. However, if you actually had an array of food laid out in front of you, your body would know more clearly, instinctively, in the moment, what to go for!

We encounter this process numerous times during a day on lots of different levels. We have to get to know our body, its energetic state and what it demands and the sensations we are actually experiencing, all beyond the images that may be played in our mind as they can be cumbersome and limited.

I remember years ago watching my mind when I unexpectedly had a day off work, and found it immediately playing the tape of what I should do with that day off, which was sit at home and watch films on my laptop, while indulging in an array of comfort foods, since this is the habit pattern which I'd most recently engaged with on a day off so it was playing through my mind! (I also had a job I found stressful at the time, hence used to rebound into this kind of 'recovery' behaviour when I had time.)

And to be fair, there was a degree of validity in the imagery as I associated it with relaxation, which part of me wanted, but so much more of me also wanted other levels of nourishment. My heart was seeking connection and my mind more subtle nourishment than my laptop! So I sat and observed as my body and instincts took command beyond that of my mind's story and started striking up conversations with my housemates (also with a much greater degree of exuberance given the introverted imagery of my mental level play) and very soon I got myself invited to a friend's place in another city and before I knew it was in my car and en route!

What was most striking about this was that what I *thought* I needed, from the story in my mind, and what I actually needed were *so* far apart!

KEY POINT

Sometimes when you are tired it's not always because you've been doing too much of something, it's because you haven't been doing enough of the things that really feed and nourish you.

So sitting at home and 'trancing out' was never, on that day, going to feed my soul like it wanted at that moment, as what I needed was feeding, not starving myself further of experiences to uplift me!

Preconceptions in relationships

While this phenomenon of preconception can apply to every moment and aspect of our lives, a particular area it can be very prominent is within our relationships with other people, since there are so many variable factors that the mind can be desperate to cling onto the familiar and reference the back catalogue of experiences already held within the body-mind. This is even more amplified with romantic relationships where our heart is more vulnerable.

While some part of you is actually aware of the array of dynamics that are really happening between you and another person, the mind tries valiantly to impose its preconceptions and memories that are stirred from previous connections in your life.

Going way back in my own personal history I well remember that whenever I was attracted to a woman I would immediately find my mind imposing its relationship template upon the situation, running it through the same expectation sequence based on previous relationships I'd had and the preconceptions I'd built up from relationships I'd witnessed earlier in my life. The previous cumbersome 'model' I would play in my head is that every woman I was attracted to could become my 'girlfriend' with all the ensuing sexual and romantic associations.

Nowadays I'm much more adept at realising that every relationship with every woman (and every person I know for that matter) is different and contains a completely different set of dynamics depending on what energy centres or chakras are activated within that relationship (see Chapter 6 on relationship dynamics), and whatever happens will be a fresh creation walking down a different path.

It's true that sometimes we might meet someone with a sense of affinity that enables an 'ongoing' relationship, but other times it's more transient in nature, with the main connecting factor being the group or collective experience you are sharing, rather than a strong personal level affinity.

I remember when a friend visited my house one night when I also had four of my female friends visiting, all of whom were particularly vibrant, soulful women. He asked about how I got on being surrounded by so many beautiful women, and whether I had to treat and categorise them all as 'sisters' in my mind as a means of handling being around them!

While being somewhat taken aback by his comments and that he couldn't see the scope for just being friends, it did actually remind me about how the mind initially works with its preconceptions. His comments reminded me that actually when I first met each of those women individually I was attracted to them and my mind did play its 'relationship tape' of perceiving how each could fit into my dream, expectations, and projection of an ongoing romantic connection, wondering if they were the 'one'. My mind still does tend to play that tape whenever I meet someone, only now I tend to listen to it a bit less, and indeed need to remind myself to wake up from its overpowering volume at times!

However, having now got to know them, I can see that with each of them there are completely different dynamics of attraction at work. Just to note, I don't deny there is attraction; I wouldn't spend time with them if there wasn't, but it's all about what the nature of the attraction is and appreciating it for what it is, not what my mind wants it to be.

And this same projection dynamic can of course also be true in any relationship, whatever the gender interplay, and wherever it exists across the spectrum of friends and lovers. Maybe you meet someone and think great, this person can be my new 'best' friend, as they remind you of a friend from the past, but again try and notice what's real and present now in the dynamics.

And to live authentically, what is actually real is of course even better than the 'mental model' as I'm alive and paying attention to the reality of what is in front of me. That's the pain and ecstasy of life – life is never the dream, but if you can fully explore the dance of what is actually happening then the reality can bring untold riches!

Essentially, just remember you are much more than the stories you play on your mental level channel. You can imagine the stories you are hearing are like the radio stuck on repeat in the background in your house while you continue to live and move around it.

Find the dancer in you!

A teacher of mine, Ya'Acov Darling Khan, co-founder of the School of Movement Medicine, often uses a phrase when he leads dance and movement workshops about finding "the dancer inside of you" and that we all "have a dancer inside"[13].

This is a great expression, which I feel really encapsulates what we are discussing with ego, instinct and preconceptions. It aligns with realising that we are more than just the stories and ego dialogue in our mind (which we can relate to as being 'who we are') and that the body has its own wisdom to move and interact with its environment independent of what the mind says.

In free spontaneous dance you are essentially practising being free and witnessing how your instinctive self moves in relation to the rhythms that are engaging with your body in a much quicker way than your ego mind can keep up with.

So this is a great practice for realising that you are more than the calculating intellect and library of memories and instead that you are a spontaneous instinctive creature who knows how to engage with what's around you.

Many has been the time, particularly if I have been dancing with someone, that I've afforded myself a wry smile or giggle as I've watched my ego mind making suggestions as to what I should 'do next' while I observe my body just spontaneously and instinctively moving totally differently, and the mind dialogue always being a split second behind in time to what is actually happening! For example, the suggestion of the mind to 'move to the left' is way behind the actual instinct which has already taken me in some other direction. This is also similar to how in conversation words come out of the mouth faster than we can think of them!

So I feel Ya'Acov's assertion to find the dancer within you encourages you not just to relate to yourself as the ego dialogue but as the bigger sense of self of who you are beyond that, that you have that spontaneous being inside you.

It changes your perception of who you are, unleashing that dancer within. It makes you realise that somewhere within that stream of dialogue of who we think we are there is also someone who can dance, move with life spontaneously and know exactly where to go and what to do next! We are in soul territory again now. And of course you practise this so that you then bring it off the dance floor into your life and live your life like that.

Of course you can also invert this notion that we have a 'dancer' inside of us, and see instead that you – the sense of self who you think you are – are actually inside a dancer. That is, the smaller sense of mind of who you think you are is actually within something much bigger, and you don't always recognise it, preferring to 'stay small' and align to the mind, rather than the bigger sense of self – the soul.

And it's important to note that dance isn't really taking you into any kind of altered perspective, it's just returning you to your naturally balanced broader One that gets skewed by the stresses of everyday life and the excessive cerebral culture and lack of embodiment that modern lifestyles encourage. Please see Chapter 7 for more on the benefits of dance for the mind and body.

Transcending the mind

Even though many spiritual and meditation systems seem intent on transcending the mind, which is great, learning to understand it is also very important as not everything which goes on in there, as I have discussed, is useless chatter, which many systems have you believe. This is the whole point: you are learning to become discerning and respectful to what goes on within you (self-respect).

Since the body and mind are connected, in the same way you wouldn't want to disown or ignore parts of your physical body, your internal chatter deserves the same reverence since it's actually just an extension of the body.

Learning to understand the terrain of the mind and understanding transcendence (which I relate to as the process of engaging with soul consciousness) are both equally as important.

Transcendence – a linear path?

It's also important to note that transcendence or enlightenment are not in some respects a linear path. We can often have the impression that the more we meditate the more enlightened we become, each day being more enlightened than the last.

Yes in one sense the more we meditate the more aware we become of when we are out of sorts and fine-tune our awareness, so there can be an underlying movement towards being more enlightened and aware.

But an enlightened or transcended moment is just that – it's a moment, or state that anyone can move into and then back out of. Even people who don't do any spiritual practices as such may have moments of enlightenment or transcendence and connection to soul, but we don't then stay there permanently in that mind state from there on!

However, obviously the more we fine-tune our self-awareness the more adept we become at knowing where we presently are in our state of being. I can feel when I'm badly out of sorts, or when I'm connected to what I interpret as my soul desire. If I hadn't cultivated such fine-tuned inner awareness this may not be possible, but it wouldn't mean that I wouldn't necessarily, like anyone else, have moments of it.

But instead of looking for a needle in a haystack, or trying to stumble around to find the light, increasing your internal awareness makes it much easier to stay keenly attuned to your path (your Tao).

Taoist?
Someone who understands the Tao does not necessarily constantly live in it moment by moment. In fact, a Taoist may often fall outside of the Tao, it's just that they use its existence as a guiding light, a beacon to try to bring themselves back into line with it.
It's about the awareness AND choosing to follow it. In that moment you are experiencing the Tao, therefore, arguably a Taoist.
Richard Brook, 2005

6

Relationship Dynamics: Understanding the Friction and Harmony

My relationship journey

Until the last few years, my intimate relationship history wasn't a good one. Not so much in respect of the relationships being tumultuous, containing malicious acts or lacking integrity, but just that in my early years and twenties there weren't many to speak of, and those that I had I found very difficult!

I attribute this to a few things, including in part the essence of what this book is all about: connection with one's own passion and joy, and how that can make you more attractive. It's not lost on me that when I jumped onto my path and started doing more of what I love in my life, natural confidence emerged, my heart radiance and presence increased, my sense of inner security increased and I suddenly found women much more interested in me. It took a while for me to get my head around this, as inside, at my core, I felt the same as when I would go months with no one seemingly being interested in me, but now people wanted to spend time with me.

Also, being very sensitive comes with its advantages and disadvantages. In some respects, it's an advantage that I tend to 'feel' more; my senses pick up more sensory input, but in some respects, it's also a disadvantage that I 'feel' more and my senses pick up more!

If someone is energetically less sensitive than me – or what we might think of as being more 'thick skinned' – I think their experience of reality can be quite different. Whereas I can feel the presence of someone really strongly who isn't even touching me (as I can feel their energetic radiance) I often think in comparison that those who are less sensitive might not feel the same intensity of connection until someone is actually touching them.

Of course, they might also still be aware of the subtleties of mood of the people around them by observing other signs – tone of voice and mannerisms – but I suspect they feel the intensity of the other person's 'energy' to a lesser extent.

My experience of relationships, alongside being trapped inside my own 'fear' for many years when I was younger, is that when I spend time with someone I can get sensitive to the point I can almost feel which chakras (see Chapter 3) on my body are expanding and contracting in relation to the other person. So, having someone in front of me that I fancied was great, but I would also feel a lot of whatever else the other person radiated, which could be tricky, as often the youthful 'male party line', where I came from anyway, would be that if someone is visually attractive you should be well up for being sexual with the person!

But since my experiences would go vastly beyond the visual, small nuances would bother me. For example, I've often in the past found it very difficult to sleep in the same bed as my partner as I'd feel that whatever they were radiating (from their energy field) would impact me and stop me from resting easily, often resulting in headaches and fatigue! And no one wants to hear you complaining each morning that you feel crap waking up next to them, particularly as it also goes against the conventional Western perspective that when you partner up with someone you share a bed.

Interestingly, I discovered whilst studying Taoism and Tantra that there are schools of thought recommending not sleeping in the same bed as your partner in order to keep the energetic polarity and thus magnetic attraction between you both. This is because it avoids their subtle energies and radiance just merging into and becoming 'welded' onto your own. Reading recommendations like that, probably written by fellow sensitives, was always music to my ears as it made me feel a bit more 'normal' but again, still a bit of a hard sell to those of a more conventional outlook!

And of course, as I alluded to earlier, my relationship woes weren't always solely about the effect of the other person's radiance on my feelings, but also relationships were tricky because of the state of my own being, chakras, emotive memories and what projections, in this case particularly 'fear', I was bringing to the relationship too. You've always got to own what you are bringing to a relationship!

And unfortunately, what I was bringing wasn't good. Being sensitive and a bit of a fish out of water generally, and not really knowing my path or what exhilarated me on a heart level, meant that a lot of the time my heart was actually quite closed. And it doesn't tend to open unless it feels safe and secure enough to do so. Given I wasn't really exercising the passion of my heart through activities in my life, which help to carry over the heart opening state into your relationships, it meant it generally stayed quite shut.

So even when I was safe and secure in my early life, the seeds of this closure were already there, not really with my family and very close friends, but if it was anything to do with girls I was attracted to, I would freeze back up. At that age I was obviously also too young to be consciously aware of these dynamics within me or how to work with them.

As I started to develop, though, the sudden exposure to 'life' and loss of the sense of security I had when my parents separated really left me in a very exposed and precarious position. Not only did I have this very vulnerable, sensitive heart, I was now feeling very insecure in virtually all other aspects of my life too. My experience now tells me it's a lot easier to welcome someone closely into your life when you have the other legs of the stool firmly anchored to the ground – in this case I felt as if I had virtually none! I was trying to find a new set of friends and emotional supporters in my life, get on with college when I didn't really know what I was doing in an ambition sense, cope with living in a different place and process the sudden change in me and my life.

It seems apt at this point to go back to my first real girlfriend whom I mentioned in the Prologue. At a time when I wasn't doing very well, I met a real shining jewel of a girl and fell in love with her. My heart felt massively opened and exposed but there was no real sense of support and security from other parts of my life for it. Cue everything falling apart.

Handling adolescent love can be difficult for most, but due to a few additional distressing events, I really buckled under and snapped shut, just unable to cope regardless of how much love and desire to connect might also have been present. So painful were the events, it took me many years to acknowledge, both to myself and the other person, how much I cared for them. The pain had etched on my heart when it snapped shut, and so not only would I not want to open it again, of course when I did, I would re-experience what was left in there from my previous experiences: unprocessed anguish.

The pain became part of the subconscious filter of how I saw relationships and what would happen when I get close to someone – why would I think any different? Pretty much the sole close experience I encountered bit me and hurt like hell, so you just think that's what's out there – pain. Once bitten, twice very shy indeed!

I couldn't get past this subconscious 'frame' for many years: in my mind I wanted each person I met to basically 'be' my ex, compared them to my ex, and wanted to play out and continue the unresolved 'stuff'.

So ingrained was her essence on my heart, I couldn't get 'past' her. When I'd meet other people and open a little that essence would then float back up from where it was in the depths of my heart chakra back to the surface too. I would despair that I wouldn't be able to get over her and move on! I did eventually, by basically acknowledging, addressing and acting on my feelings, as I felt like my life was slipping away if I didn't. So eventually I expressed what I was feeling to her, though it was too late by then (it was a few years later) but I didn't mind so much as I had answered the inner calling of my heart instead of trying to suppress it and that was what was important!

Anyway, this was a pretty deep wound I had, and probably still to some degree affects me today when I get very close to someone, such is the way things like this become part of your perspective. But since then I've also had some really great relationships too, so it isn't all bad!

Part of my development, and what started to help immensely, was beginning to understand how each person I met affected me differently. This would help me escape the dreaded 'template' or 'model' of how I thought a relationship 'should' be. Learning more about chakras and vibration (I was especially inspired by the work of Zulma Reyo and Osho around sexuality, tantra and chakra polarities[14]), I started to realise that each person would naturally trigger something different in me, and it didn't make it 'wrong'. I think you are either conditioned to compare everyone to your early loves, or against the model we are societally exposed to through mass media such as Hollywood, and I guess I was no different. My mind would have a really hard time weighing up what 'category' I should place a new-found acquaintance into: 'Is this person a friend, or a lover?'

Understanding chakra dynamics in relationships helped me to see that each person essentially triggers a different combination of thoughts, feelings and physical instincts in you depending what chakras they resonate with and trigger in you. I then gave up trying to compare people I'd be intimate with to either each other or the mass media ideal.

I just see them as different – simple. Some people might trigger my heart more, some my sexual desire more, some my mind more, some my voice more, some my desire to be nurtured more, and the millions of permutations in between! Seeing relationships in this light is also one of the key ideas I impart to my patients who similarly devour this information with great relish. It's also very handy to remember that chakra dynamics are actually in play in all our relationships, not just our romantic ones, but each person we meet triggers different combinations within us. It just is what it is – as my brother likes to remind me. (He has such wisdom without having to work it all out like me!)

Nuts and Bolts: Tutorial

Relationship dynamics can be tremendously challenging at times, trying to make sense of the myriad of apparently contradictory feelings of connection and disconnection, friction and harmony, which can abound when you get close to another person. Your head can be left spinning trying to figure out what is going on!

It's also not helped by the lack of accessible and common language to express how we feel – we don't usually get taught in school how to express feelings let alone break down the subtlety of our human experience.

However, fortunately, in my exploration of all things holistic I've found that understanding two relatively basic concepts, the nature of vibration and the chakra system – both of which we touched on earlier – allows a quick and simple way to understand what can otherwise seem like the complex dynamics of relationships.

So before continuing further here's a reminder of some of the key points around vibration:

KEY POINTS: REMINDERS

All phenomena are made up of vibration, on a range from the more dense vibrations such as those that make up your physical body, to the lighter more subtle vibrations, such as those that make up your thoughts.

Those vibrations in the human body are particularly felt and expressed in what we call chakras - which are essentially seven main nerve plexuses, which span the full spectrum of faculties we have as a human being from our physical body and the Earth beneath us through to our thoughts and feelings and connection to the Space above us.

In terms of how we experience vibration, the easiest way to recognise the importance and tangible effect of vibrations is through using music as an example, as it's a source of vibration that we can readily relate to.

Depending on the vibrational qualities of the music, you can be aware and feel it more readily in different parts of the body. In addition, it can also have such significant impact it can catalyse physical movement in you (which you experience when you dance) and it can attract, repel or have a neutral impact on you.

So taking this awareness that everything we engage with is comprised of vibration, it also means that everything we engage with also actually affects and influences us. And of course, fundamental to this chapter is the point that other people give off vibrations!

And just like with music, we feel other people's vibration through our body, through our nerves – our chakras. And we can also similarly experience that full spectrum of reactions of being energised, feeling neutral or repelled, and that is happening for each chakra which is why there are so many unique dynamics at play with each person you meet!

Your own vibration and chemistry

What's also key is that we all of course radiate vibrations ourselves, which people can similarly react to, and that each relationship dynamic with each person you meet is completely unique, as no two people have the same subtle vibrations. You could have 100 people stand in front of you and each would experience your presence in a slightly different way depending on what happens when the two energy fields (your and their vibrations) interact.

As we also discussed in Chapter 3, this unique interaction and alchemy of energy fields coming together creates what we think of as 'chemistry'. When you engage with another person you both become more than the sum of your individual selves as a third 'energy' is born, that which is created from your energy fields interacting, which those present get to be bathed in and experience. This is the beauty (and sometimes the heartache!) of relating, that you both get to experience an energy that feels so personal but actually belongs to no one.

As an analogy, it would be like taking the singular sound of two musical instruments, and observing what gets created when you combine the two – sometimes a very different new sound which then also permeates the experience of the musicians.

We will discuss this dynamic of 'chemistry' a little more later in this section too.

How people 'rub off' on us

Sometimes we also absorb vibrations from other people into our chakras and body tissues, which is why we can still feel the presence of the person with us after they may no longer be in close physical proximity. Literally other people do 'rub off' on us, and we also absorb this magical 'chemistry' into our system too, so the energetic chemistry which we create together can also remain for a while after as well.

Similarly, the sentiment that we often express when someone irritates us, that they are 'getting on our nerves', is actually a totally accurate appraisal of the situation, since it is your nerves that are getting irritated by the other person!

But just remember that since we all radiate a slightly different set of subtle vibrations it might well be that someone else may not feel that same reaction, since the 'chemistry' can be unique to one particular relationship.

However, it would also be remiss not to acknowledge our own role in what we experience in life and relationships by attempting to keep our own vibration and radiance in good harmony. So while it's true that each relationship dynamic is unique, it's also wise to consider what you may be radiating and how it's influencing the situation.

Let's revisit our situation where you have 100 people standing in front of you. While we identified that each person might experience you in a slightly different way, it can still have a similar 'theme'. If you are predominantly radiating negativity and overall discordance, this will still be the underlying expression even if it comes across and is interpreted differently by each person. Just as bad, out of tune music will still sound like bad, out of tune music to most who hear it!

Similarly, if you are radiating beautiful harmonious vibrations, it will still be the underlying energy which makes contact with the other person, even if the interaction of the two energy fields and the other person's own 'filter' can skew it somewhat.

So, in alignment with the rest of the teachings here, increasing your self-awareness of what you are radiating will also help you begin to understand when you are coming out of balance, and the therapeutic practices we discuss in Chapter 7 will help to bring you back to balance.

As this work explains, I promote yoga and therapies as a wonderful way to alleviate stress from the body, but it's also equally as important to be doing what you love and be as passionate about your life as possible. When you do what you love, as we have previously discussed it increases the radiance of your subtle heart vibration which has the dual impact of positively benefitting the other organs in your body – which helps harmonise your entire vibration and helps you to be more attractive to be around!

Dynamics of close relationships

Having identified that each person is radiating a particular set of vibrations which can elicit a range of responses, we can now delve a little deeper into the specifics of the dynamics you may experience with another person.

In essence, since we are dealing with the dynamics of seven different centres, there are a myriad of combinations of chakra resonance or discordance that can happen in relationship with another person. These dynamics can happen to a degree in any interaction, but can be more significantly engaged and triggered in the intimacy of a close relationship.

As we touched on above, with each person you engage with, for each chakra, it can respond across the entire spectrum: it may be energised or excited, sit in a neutral or harmonious resonance, or be agitated (abraded) with. Friction or irritation as we often call it. This is why with any one person we can experience – often simultaneously – a sense of connection, excitation and irritation! It all exists within the energy field between you and the other person at the same moment, and what comes to the surface can depend on which chakras are being triggered most or are in the 'energetic ascendancy' at any one time.

Let's look at some detailed examples. You might experience around someone a great degree of excitation in the first and second chakra which means there would be a lot of sexual desire, but at the same time you might have an abrasion (friction) at the sixth chakra (the third eye) which means that you might see the world very differently and have conflict around it. So when you are in a sexual dynamic with your partner, and those chakras are in the ascendancy, then you may feel very connected, but while debating life perspectives you may feel the connection becomes conflicted.

Or for example, you may have your heart chakra in a state of excitation, so when you see each other you feel lots of love and warmth, but if the throat chakra doesn't resonate you might struggle to communicate and have fluid conversation.

Learn and observe which chakras are triggered in relationships

A particularly helpful exercise I've often suggested to my patients is to look at which chakras are mainly triggered in particular relationships. Seeing relationship dynamics in this light can help to stop us from falling into judgement around our relationships, as there isn't really a right and wrong or 'black and white' of relationship dynamics, just the dance of what actually gets triggered between you.

It can also help the mind to relax a little bit to gain this perspective, as the mind always likes clear black and white opinion on what a relationship *should* look like, and what 'category' a particular relationship falls into – also partly built into our collective consciousness through all the Hollywood imagery we are fed which depicts relationships in a particular light. For example, the mind likes to categorise that someone is either a boyfriend or girlfriend which comes with a relatively fixed set of ideas of how that should be, or the mind likes to think the person is just a friend, again with a set of ideas of how that should be. But as we are identifying, in reality, there are so many different permutations that could be present within a relationship dynamic, as there are so many shades of grey!

Chakra qualities in relationships

It's useful at this point to give a brief overview of general chakra qualities and how they manifest when triggered in relationships so you can consider which chakras may have been strongly stimulated within particular relationships you have had.

Note: The qualities below relate to when a chakra is positively stimulated. If there is a neutral response in the relationship you won't feel much different than you usually do, or if they are actually agitated or abraded with you would actually feel that aspect of you close, contract, be irritated, repelled or come into conflict.

Table 5: Chakra qualities in relationships

Base chakra resonance	Sense of feeling secure in your body, and flowing in sexual expression
Sacral chakra resonance	Sense of feeling physically connected and intimately relaxed and close
Solar plexus chakra resonance	Sense of being able to express yourself, be respected and have equal and appropriate use of power in the relationship
Heart chakra resonance	Sense of love and compassion
Throat chakra resonance	Sense of ability to communicate fluidly and truthfully
Third eye chakra resonance	Sense of accurate perception and intuition with each other
Crown chakra resonance	Sense of connection to the greater whole, in addition to your partner

It may also be useful to refer to the Chakra Associations chart in Chapter 3, which also gives indications as to what can be stimulated in you when a particular chakra is activated.

Examples of chakra dynamics in relationships

I've drawn out a few of the key chakra characteristics, resonances and abrasions from a couple of people I've had particularly close relationships with. Let's call the first person 'Charlotte'. The first chakra felt very slightly activated, so there was a moderate degree of sexual charge, but the second chakra felt strongly activated so I felt very at home and comfortable with this person. There was a strong competitive dynamic between us meaning that the third chakra was slightly abrasive against each other. Interestingly, the third chakra sits above the liver, which in Chinese medicine is associated with our ability to assert ourselves and our direction in life.

This can go some way to explaining why this energy centre can have an edge of competitiveness about it, and why if it's in friction with another person it can result in both wanting to assert themselves over the other. The fourth (heart) centre resonated well with feelings of genuine non-conditional love, as did the fifth centre, so communication was easy, and I would also say there was a strong spiritual correlation in the higher centres, so that we felt on the same wavelength, attuned to similar subtle vibrations of energy.

Alternatively, when I was engaging with 'Liz' I felt a huge amount of sexual charge, meaning the base chakra was very stimulated, but I wouldn't actually feel so comfortable just hanging out with this person; the sense of comfort in my belly wasn't great, so the second chakra was off resonance. Indeed, I'd often find my legs tightening up when I was with them as I felt off centre in their presence, and my legs were trying to grip onto the Earth to provide a sense of security. There was no competitiveness, so ease at the third chakra, but there was a very strongly activated fourth (heart) centre with huge feelings of love towards her. With Liz there was also a tremendous ease of communication, so the fifth chakra was strongly resonant, and interestingly when I communicated with those I actually felt my head and neck craning back slightly as if to open my throat and allow out the words I'd be longing to speak from the deeper levels of my being, from my heart. And there was also a strong sense of spiritual correlation from the higher centres.

As you can see there are often a number of different forces at work within any one dynamic with another person. I'd hasten to add that the two pictures above both sound fairly good – of course they were which is why I chose to get close to these women as there was a lot of resonance, as we usually tend to pursue the relationships with more resonance! There are also plenty of examples I could also give of connections with people which had much more discordance, but I'd generally assess these dynamics pretty quickly, realising there was very little common ground and so less attraction to explore!

Sometimes the only common frequency (common ground) we may have with another person is that we share a common field of consciousness – for example we may work in the same setting as someone – so we share that same perceptual context. This is a third eye resonance of sharing a mutual perspective but there may be little else outside of that context. Equally sometimes we know people who seem to irritate us on virtually every level!

If you reflect on your relationships and see particular patterns consistently coming to the fore it can also be an indicator of how your own chakras are particularly inherently charged. This can also help us understand what qualities we are bringing to a relationship and impacting those we are close to.

Feel through all your senses

We may not be used to perceiving our relationships with the degree of subtlety we've been discussing, for a number of reasons.

Sometimes it's because we've not been introduced to this area of chakra dynamics, so we haven't had a 'framework' in which to reference, explore or consciously make sense of our experiences.

Other times it can also be because our subtle 'energy body' has hardened up, become dense or closed, and we experience life in a grosser sensory reality where subtle energetics may not be detectable to our conscious mind. In this respect again, yoga, therapies and time in nature all make you a bit more aware and are useful practices for building up your sensitivity.

It's also useful to increase awareness of our relationships using this perspective, as a common trait we can also have is to visually judge people, particularly in romantic relationships, and give excessive precedence to what we see. While you can't stop the mind making commentary on what you observe, the mistake would be in overemphasising and drawing rash conclusions from it when, as we have discovered, it's such a small part of the overall experience we have when we connect with someone.

Feeling through your chakras

Given our tendency of visually judging people, it's useful to try getting in proximity with someone and working your awareness through your chakras and seeing how you feel in each of them. See if you can work out which ones may be more activated/opened or which ones may be shying away and wanting to close to protect themselves. This can be detectable through your physical body, or through the associated feeling or action that comes from each chakra.

For example, if you stand next to someone and feel a sexual charge your lower centres are activated, or if you feel like giving them a hug your heart is open. Or you may feel like talking – obviously in this case you may not be able to discern that the physiology of the throat feels any different, but the feeling to readily talk tells you it's open. Conversely, if you stand next to someone and feel like closing your chest there may be heart friction, or if you don't feel you can communicate freely the throat chakra is closed.

Exercise: Feel through your chakras

You can do this exercise with a range of people at different levels of proximity, but evidently, if you are placing yourself in intimately close proximity to someone, make sure it's ok and appropriate to do so!

Take notice of which chakras are triggered in three different scenarios: a) with a lover, b) with a friend, c) with a stranger you engage with.

You can notice which chakras might be particularly triggered, in the moment, by observing the following:

a) Changes in the area of your body corresponding to each chakra: e.g. sexual arousal, relaxation of the belly, opening of the chest, desire to reach out, throat opening, spine straightening and crown of head craning upwards (crown chakra stimulation). There is also of course the converse of each of these which can be a closing of these areas.

b) If the physical cues appear too subtle, notice what feelings, emotions, desires and inclinations are activated e.g.

- feelings of sexual stimulation
- feelings of security or insecurity, relaxation or fear
- sense of harmony/competitiveness
- sense of warmth and desire to reach out or contract and move away
- desire to talk or feel shut down
- sense of being on the same wavelength and understanding each other or feeling separate
- sense of shared connection to the broader spiritual nature of life or disconnected from that

The perfect relationship?

Exercises like the above ones are also useful to try and snap us out of our ideas surrounding the 'perfect relationship'. If you contemplate that you are receiving input from all seven chakras simultaneously, some of which may resonate and some which may be abrasive to you, then it stands a good chance that the possibility of meeting someone where all seven energy centres resonate perfectly with our own, all the time, is fairly limited!

If it seems all a bit too complex to review relationships in this light of seven different sets of dynamics, you may just want to work with three levels, roughly sexual attraction (do you fancy the other person), heart feeling (do you naturally open to this person and feel affectionate) and mental level resonance (do you think similarly). Even working with three levels can help to sort out some of the chaos of how our mind perceives relationships.

Internal conflict and imbalance in relationship

We can also inhibit input and awareness from our chakras through either distracting ourselves and keeping our attention elsewhere, or 'locking' our spine (see also Chapter 7). This relates to not only avoiding the energetic radiance from another person close to you, or from a vibration we've previously absorbed into our system (when someone or something has 'rubbed off' on us and impacted us greatly), but also avoiding hearing the intelligence of one particular chakra as it conflicts with what another is experiencing!

For example, we discussed how when engaging with another person we received simultaneous input through all chakras. In this situation, it could be that we have a very strong heart chakra resonance, but that a vibration at another centre, such as the base chakra, could be particularly abrasive. So what we would be experiencing would be feeling heart opening feelings of love coupled with a feeling of insecurity and lack of a sense of ease of being comfortably 'grounded' around the person, which would then create a confused and conflicting mental picture (like a lot of relationships do!).

However, on the whole, it may be that the feelings of nourishment for the heart outweigh the sense of insecurity, so overall we've got a picture where we choose to stay in close relationship. But those sensations of insecurity are still there; the base chakra will still be indicating its lack of comfort with the situation, so to avoid internally 'hearing' that feedback you may choose to distract yourself with other sensory stimulation (where's the chocolate?!) or lock down the feedback from that chakra by creating tension in that part of the physiology by locking the spine, creating tension in that area to try and numb the sensations and avoid experiencing them internally via the mind.

An alternative is also that we may consciously compensate, by doing lots of grounding practices while in close relationship with this person to rebalance our own energies, and indeed, the relationship could also in fact be highlighting that we have an internal imbalance in this chakra, leaving us susceptible to coming out of balance, which healing techniques also help. So in this circumstance it's not the relationship so much that is creating the imbalance, more that it's highlighting an imbalance that exists within you!

I'm not advocating that you avoid relationships which create these kind of conflicting dynamics, as they abound by the very nature of how relationships operate. I'm just explaining the mechanism of how they happen so you can understand and be conscious of the reality as it is! People have different vibrations than we do ourselves, which is why we are drawn to more closely relate to them as it also nourishes us, but within those dynamics are these other intricacies and abrasions which can create the friction we've discussed. Ultimately, remember it's our heart and soul that is the supreme controller of our actions, and they choose to keep us in situations that are ultimately for the highest benefit of all concerned. So, as I advocate, keep your heart and soul in the ascendancy, and your awareness of their inner voice primed!

Making love

We touched in Chapter 3 on the dynamics of relationship 'chemistry', which can also explain the phenomenon of what we refer to in a relationship context as 'making love'.

Energy fields interacting in an ascendant heartfelt manner create an incredibly beautiful, neutral and abundant energy field, connected to the essence of creation itself – love – that those present are bathed in, but which 'belongs' to no one! It is literally the combination of the individuals' energies merged together that essentially create and amplify a feeling of 'love' – which is a beautiful, neutral but abundant energy field that nourishes all life.

Please note, although we often relate to making love as being an overtly physical, sexual interaction with genital contact, it doesn't have to be. It's the nature of the interaction of the energy fields which is significant. Of course, there are many unique kinds of chemistry, where this magical 'third element' is created that you both get to experience. With some people a chemistry of humour, fun, playfulness, creativity or sensuality can emerge and so on!

Chakra polarities in men and women

The last area I am going to visit in this section on relating is chakra polarities. In regard to relationship dynamics it goes a long way to helping our understanding of different gender characteristics and perspectives.

So while chakra qualities (such as those described in Chapter 3) have a general similarity in both sexes (such as that the base chakra relates to our connection with the Earth and the crown to our higher states of perception), they also have an inherent polarity difference related to gender.

It's important to add that I'm conscious there are many different identifiable gender categorisations, but for the purposes and clarity of this work we are identifying what are seen as the archetypal masculine and feminine polarities. However this does not mean that each person has these exact clearly defined chakra polarities related to their biological sex. Clearly there are many gender configurations across the spectrum of humanity that we are now becoming more understanding of.

As you can identify from Image 9, each chakra on each gender expresses itself with an opposing polarity to that of the opposite gender.

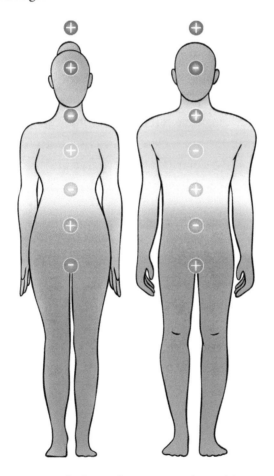

Image 9: Chakra polarities in male and female

For example, the base chakra on a male gender has a positive charge, and the female a negative, and then each chakra alternates polarity – and thus has the opposite charge to the other gender – all the way through to the crown chakra (which shares the same polarity, as on that level, we are all One).

You could also observe that these chakra differences are generally mirrored within the difference in each sex's physiology, notwithstanding gender variances as acknowledged above. For example, we can observe that the masculine base chakra has a positive polarity and is accompanied by a lingam (penis) that extends away from the body and the male is more inclined to positively express himself from this chakra, whereas the yoni (vagina) of the feminine is a negative (receptive) chakra, and receives inwardly. So we can see a clear distinction between the yang, masculine positive polarity, at that chakra and that of the yin, female negative receptive polarity, at that chakra.

You can also see this again quite clearly at the second chakra which is positive for the feminine, and within the area of the body the female has the additional reproductive organs (womb, ovaries) as compared to the male. And again, with the heart chakra that is positive for the female, and we can see the pronounced breast as compared to the male. The physiological differences aren't so pronounced with the other chakras, but the polarities still oppose in exactly the same way.

However, alongside the physical level differences, the mental and emotional aspects of each gender are also influenced by the opposing polarities, which combined together significantly influence the way that each gender relates to their experience of life.

Essentially our chakra polarities become part of the filter

that we see the world through and go some way to explaining why different genders perceive the world in different ways. When we begin to understand this, we can then also appreciate the different vantage points of each gender instead of thinking they should see things 'our' way! For example, it means that women deal with the mental world in a different way than men, and men deal with the emotional world differently than women.

And the opposing polarities are also very evident when we look at close intimate and sexual relationships, and how they influence how we perceive and relate. As men have a positive polarity at the base chakra, they tend to be more sexually 'yang' and assertive from this chakra whereas women are more 'yin' receptive into that chakra.

Since we see the world through the 'filter' of our own chakra polarities, men often can't understand why women aren't also so sexually driven from their base chakra. Whereas women, who are used to being receptive in that chakra, think that men are too driven from there! However, the converse is true for the heart chakra. As it's a positive chakra for women, it influences how they relate more from the heart, and then also think men should as well, but it's a receptive chakra for men so naturally they don't assert their energy or perception from there in the same way.

So the phenomenon of chakra polarities goes some way to explaining why people can struggle to grasp and relate to where the other is coming from, as naturally you have a different perception. Both partners want intimacy and connection; it just expresses differently and understanding this is actually ultimately helpful of course, as it enables you to be more accepting of the inherent differences.

As regards these differences in expression created by chakra polarities, it's also fascinating that we often acknowledge and more readily accept (and admire) the physical level differences between the sexes and the sense of beauty on that level, but we don't as readily accept the inherent emotional and mental differences. For example, you don't often hear someone comment about the opposite sex that they wished they looked more like their own sex, but we quite often hear comments regarding the mental and emotional functioning of the opposite sex wishing it was more like that of their own!

However, and here's the crux of it, the two sets of chakra polarities ultimately balance each other. In partnership, bringing together the positive and negative qualities of each chakra ultimately creates a balanced whole which each person can experience while together with someone that isn't possible in the same way on your own.

Additionally, the more we can sit in our positive polarities, the more it allows each partner to receive and be nourished into their receptive chakras. You actually make love and have connection through all chakras, which is where we have often gone awry in our understanding of intimate connection.

It's also important to note that your own chakra polarities can become even more polarised when in relationship with someone of opposing gender characteristics. This means that when you come into relationship with a member of the opposite sex, your positive chakras can promote themselves even more, and the negative ones can become even more receptive.

So being around the opposite polarity can enable you to sit even more fully in your own 'power'. Yin and yang always seek to balance one another, so when you are single, and devoid of much contact with the opposite sex, you tend to have to blend your own masculine and feminine traits to a degree in order to stay balanced. But when someone of the opposite sex comes along, they can provide the yin to your yang and vice versa so you can open and promote your positive chakras and your partner's energy balances you.

It's a bit of a cliché but I'm reminded of the phrase often associated with relationships where the woman may say the connection 'made me feel like a woman' or the man may say the connection 'made me feel like a man' as you can sit in your own positive polarities more.

Connection is all about these polarities – it creates chemistry and 'charge' when these masculine and feminine energies engage and we sit fully in our power. Think of how a battery operates: it has two opposing polarities which together generate electrical force. Even in our everyday language we often talk of the 'electricity' within a connection and indeed this is a fairly accurate description of what happens! So, when we are in relationship and in our power, it can create an incredible fusion that energises and ascends each individual beyond that which they experience when they are alone. This indeed is part of the essence of tantric intimacy for those who wish to explore more.

Gender identities

As I touched upon earlier, in the modern world, in some respects it can now be seen more clearly that we have started to realise that gender and sex can be two distinctly different things. I've provided the basic outline of the two masculine and feminine polarity archetypes in quite a defined and distinct way but of course in reality we have variances. Some men may have chakras which rather than being distinctly positive may actually tend to be more negative and vice versa, and similarly for women too, which is why we actually have so many variations of gender characteristics and types. So the broad range of gender identities is reflective of the spectrum of polarity possibilities that each person can express.

In this respect, each person is unique, since as explained above to some degree they hold a unique set of chakra characteristics, and each person, in an ideal world, would feel wholly free to express themselves for who they are.

However, what tends to confuse this area somewhat further is that people tend to identify with and relate from their idea (which is often imbalanced) of how men and women *should* be, without understanding what the actual genuine energetic differences are.

The feminine gender can start to lean into and 'push' into their masculine as we have such an endemic patriarchal society that can seem to reward male characteristics – just look at the pay disparity and gender ratio at the top of many big businesses. This subconsciously anchors a viewpoint that in order to be successful you have to promote your masculine qualities.

By contrast the more feminine qualities, which naturally include a more positive expression of heart energy, are often kept away from big business, since it softens the masculine, and catalysing a more compassionate perspective can sometimes be bad for business! In addition to that, jobs that actively involve more feminine characteristics are often lower paid, so we are really living in an imbalanced energetic arena that can influence our perception and expression from an early age, unless we consciously become aware of it.

A converse of this is where men become somewhat ashamed or nullified as to their more 'yang' sexuality as it generates such a 'bad press'! The fact that men are so driven to intimately relate from the base chakra in particular is given a difficult time; women can perceive this as an uncouth male who is 'just after one thing' but this is also in part because it's become so distorted in media with the objectification of women on the physical level. Since the base chakra is the one with the densest vibration and it's a positive chakra for a male, it explains the greater focus of the male with the more physical, sexual level of relating. All people want connection; it just manifests in different ways!

To summarise, your identity and dispositions really come from the charge and characteristics of your chakras, not from an idea of what you think you should be. Be yourself.

Projection and energy 'cords' in relationships

We also project our desires in our own mind depending on our own chakra configuration. As we noted earlier, for example, a male may project his desire to be intimate based upon his own positive chakra configuration.

And in this instance, the high intensity sexual charge from the base chakra can also fuel and influence the projections from the chakras that sit above it. So for example, if the male has at some point allowed his receptive heart chakra to open and received the essence of a female's heart vibration (that she naturally radiates from that centre) then whenever the male gets significantly aroused, the burning fire from the base chakra projects up through and illumines (gives light to) the female energy that is currently sitting in his heart –

thus creating a strong projection towards that person that he wishes to direct his base chakra advances towards!

The strong energy from the base chakra also illumines other receptive centres, as the receptive centres tend to flip open to receive once the positive ones are activated – which is why when we get 'turned on' and push into our positive polarities we tend to more strongly desire the presence of the opposite gender to balance us. Basically we will be running a lot of our own 'charge' and it needs balancing!

Similarly for a female, when she desires connection, a strong charge passes through the heart centre (positive chakra), and if she also has received some male vibrational essence into her receptive base chakra (that he naturally radiates from that chakra) then her heart's desire will illumine the male's essence which is in her base chakra, creating a strong desire and projection towards that person that she wishes to direct her heart chakra advances towards.

Of course this dynamic of projection also works similarly through all the other receptive chakras where you may have absorbed the energy of another person. So alongside seeking out a more sexual level of intimacy with them, we may just find ourselves just 'thinking' about them, desiring to speak with them, wanting a hug from them and so on depending which chakra has absorbed their essence. Basically, whatever chakra the other person's essence is sitting in, when that chakra is stimulated there will be a projection towards that other person.

See the Chakra Associations tables earlier in this chapter and Chapter 3 for a reminder of the more detailed breakdown of each chakra's characteristics.

It's also worth noting here that we can create subtle, etheric energy cords with people we have been intimate with (on all levels, not just sexual, but friends and family and so on), particularly in sexual relationships, because the forces involved are so strong these projections can travel with great force along the cords and basically re-energise whatever karma you have with that person. This is also in part why we can find it so difficult to separate from those who we've had longstanding intimate and sexual relations with; our own projections tie cords to the other that can take quite a while to disperse and 'untether'!

For more on relationships please visit this blog: Relationships: Resistance, Commitment, Perspectives and Ties[xi]

Exercises: Chakra dynamics in your relationships

1. Reflect on three of your close, intimate relationships (the closer you are to someone the more apparent the chakra dynamics are). Go through each of the chakras and note down whether you feel the chakra is a) positively stimulated/excited, b) having a neutral/inert response or c) in a state of friction.

2. Take notice of patterns, as they can potentially be indicative of your own chakra configuration. For example, if in each relationship you have a strong heart connection, it can be indicative that your heart chakra is generally open and pronounced. Or for example, if each relationship lacks a sexual charge it can also be a sign that your base and second chakra isn't so pronounced. If you see patterns, then you could also reflect on more of your relationships to see if those patterns are reinforced further.

---

xi   www.creativewellness.co.uk/bookblogs

7

Time to Heal

My healing journey

I discovered meditation through a friend, when I was about 16. My initial engagement was with Buddhism and transcendental meditation. While initially it fascinated me as a bit of a 'quick win' way of changing my state – not a bad thing as I was fairly up and down within myself at the time – I wasn't really that taken with it all! Whether it's because I didn't particularly resonate with the practices we were exploring, or I was just too young to appreciate it, I'm not sure.

I only really got seriously hooked during a summer of work and travel around the USA when I was around 18. I did a trip called a 'Green Tortoise' which was a hippy/new age bus journey from San Francisco to New York taking 10 days. During the journey we stopped at Native American reservations and sat around campfires and slept under the stars, went hiking, rafting and all kinds of fun and nourishing stuff!

All the seats on the bus folded down, to make it into one giant mattress, so some nights we all slept together on the bus as we travelled which was great. Now this journey *was* life changing for me. It was also the first engagement I had with energywork after I witnessed the bus driver giving 'reiki' or some variant of energywork to one of my fellow travellers (which isn't something you'd generally see on the 126 service from Dudley to Birmingham where I grew up!). I became fascinated and asked him to do the same for me. He actually said he was too tired initially, but I persisted and wow am I grateful that I did!

I still mark that experience as a real turning point for me, as it was really the first time I became aware of myself beyond the confines of my physical body, that I am something bigger than that, my 'energy body'. I mean, he wasn't even touching me but I felt so much! I also feel that session was some sort of catalyst or 'opening experience' where my 'crown chakra' opened for the first time and connected me to a much larger intelligence also beyond my more regular idea of 'self'.

I'm taking care here to try not to run away into metaphysical talk that doesn't make sense, so I'll try and keep it tangible! What I mean by opening my crown chakra is that the energy centre at the top of the head, when opened or stimulated correctly, connects us to the aspect of us that plugs into the collective consciousness and a source of 'light' that goes beyond the more physical confines of time and space.

In some respects, every thought and possibility floats around in the subtle ether above us, and the crown chakra, when in tune, has an ability to act a bit like an antenna and allow us to be aware of and tune into that very expansive collective energy above us, which eventually, as it becomes more and more refined, merges back into pure light – the source of all!

The collective etheric consciousness is just one dimension or frequency of our human experience (for example the physical plane is another, the emotional plane is another – all equally as important). So you could think of the various aspects of your human 'being' as different densities of that light – at the top is the most refined, pure light, and as it gets denser and denser you eventually end up with solid physical form. Each level needs feeding equally to keep us whole and well, but I'd venture to say that while a great deal of us try our utmost to feed our more physical level, it's not so often we tune into that most subtle refined light which, since it cascades down through every other level, also then actually feeds the other levels too!

So it's not a stretch to say I never felt the same after that energywork treatment. Something had shifted in me; something opened that expanded me in a way that shaped my sense of direction from that point on. It reminds me of a saying I read once regarding spiritual practice, that "once you have tasted the light, there is no turning back".

This felt particularly true to me; something felt so powerful and peaceful, but yet also simple, that once I'd tasted it, it was drawing me towards it from that day forth.

What engaged my attention in particular regarding meditation and yoga practice was seeing and witnessing the people who I was travelling with who mentioned they did it. There was something about the way they carried themselves, something they radiated that grabbed my attention. I remember observing one girl sitting opposite me; she had her eyes closed, but I could see she wasn't asleep, as there was a fullness, aliveness and 'concentration' about her which left a lasting impression on me. She was present and full, yet seemingly resting and peaceful at the same time. Now I never asked her whether she was meditating; I don't think I needed too, but I'm sure that was what she was doing. When you meditate – particularly a physically focused one where your attention is in your body – it creates an immense amount of presence as you are concentrating your essence and awareness within your body and it increases your radiance.

I overheard the same girl talking to the bus driver about yoga and how it made her feel 'so energised' and there was just something grabbing my attention that I couldn't ignore and I was hooked on finding out more.

This tangible effect I could see on people was part of the reason why I had become much more attracted to finding out about these practices than I was a couple of years earlier. They all felt like 'impressive' people, kind, generous, peaceful, even-tempered and relaxed, whereas my earlier experiences had come through a friend showing me transcendental meditation – so I was already familiar with his qualities – and a Buddhist teacher who I didn't really resonate with.

In fact, I've got to be honest that I also felt something seemed a bit inauthentic about that particular Buddhist teacher. I remember him once telling us that you should smile no matter what. That doesn't make sense to me! I'd rather smile because I feel joy and happiness and be equally as authentic if other emotions are naturally at the fore, as they also serve a purpose! So that was a big difference. I'd seen these people in a real-life setting, and liked what I saw, whereas the previous engagement was almost like a classroom, theoretical scenario.

As soon as I got back to the UK, I made a beeline straight for university yoga classes and anything holistic related – tai chi, meditation, breathwork, shiatsu. I was lucky enough to meet my first real teacher at this point, John Wilson (my tai chi teacher in Manchester – highly recommended!), who then went on to introduce me to ceremonial dances like Sun Moon Dances and several other practices.

What I really liked about John was that he showed me again that it's still possible to be 'you', your grounded personality self, with a sense of humour, and also do these spiritual things. Originally, I'd garnered some kind of opinion that you somehow had to be perfect and holier than thou, perhaps also because I was having difficulties accepting certain aspects of myself. This has always been a theme for me, this merging of being 'spiritual' with being 'me' – Richard from Dudley who also likes football, WWE wrestling and has a mischievous sense of humour.

And what I realise now is that in essence, when a practice is being integrated correctly, there is no distinction; an effective 'spiritual' practice makes you a more effective and real human being aligned to your creative potential. It's not about surfing above your humanity, more about embracing it.

But in my early days I was still struggling with this, often using spiritual practices as a way of trying to escape my earthbound feelings and desires. It took me a while to see it's not the way. Also any good, efficacious practice actually won't 'naturally' let you do this, as the strength of the practice is in making you whole.

So for example, if you are too 'earthbound', too stuck in feelings and desires and acting them out without balanced perspective, then a practice that expands you and connects you into a broader, more spacious state of being is what you need. But for me it was the opposite. I was already trying to suppress, deny, disconnect and disengage from my thoughts and feelings, so I didn't need to drift any further towards space!

This is why I found embodied practices such as yoga and dance and movement to be particularly powerful for me, as they don't let you escape. If you are running away from your feelings, those kinds of practices help you to embrace them, make you more spontaneous and develop discernment and wisdom about impulses – this was my path. At first, I wondered why doing these practices was actually at times making me feel worse and life seemed an even greater struggle, until I realised that it was just highlighting how much I was fighting my humanity and trying to stay passive.

My ego, fear, ideas and preconceptions about who I thought I should be and what I should do were running wild, and the embodied practices – including body-centred meditations – were bringing me back into contact with my authentic feelings, and things like dance in particular enabled the spontaneity to return to me, so it all became less of an internal struggle.

Gabrielle Roth, founder of 5Rhythms Dance, says in one of her books that the practice helps you break free of a state she calls "trizophrenia" where you are "saying yes, feeling no and acting out maybe"[15]. For me this is perfectly put, as embodied practices help to pull you back into alignment, so actions, thoughts and feelings are congruent. The key point is that when you are in alignment, it's not just that you are getting inner impulses and visions and ideas, it's also that the spontaneity returns to your actions!

When I realised the initial struggle I was experiencing

was me fighting against my own humanity, fighting against the creative impulse of life, life then became easier, and bit by bit I started to learn to trust what I felt inside and the impulses that would come. I had a couple of main ways of accessing this deeper me, through the deep relaxation I would have at the end of a yoga class, by which time my 'left brain' conscious mind would have shut up enough for me to hear my heart and my right brain deeper intelligence, and also similarly while dancing I would seemingly open to deeper wisdom inside to guide me.

And when I saw that acting on these impulses appeared to keep my life moving forward in a positive, healing and creative direction, I realised I was tapping into a level of intelligence way beyond the 'other' part of my mind I would often experience when in a more 'normal' state of mind – which had developed for the most part to protect me from life rather than embrace it! That other part of my mind is usually full of predicting the future based on the past, which of course isn't very creative, is it, since creation unfurls in new, often unique directions as everything is in a constant state of unique evolution and change!

Different therapies also obviously work on different levels of me. Sometimes I feel that I need a one-to-one session with my own acupuncturist, which isn't just a 'physical' therapy as I get to share with him what's going on in my life (very much a feature of the type of acupuncture that I also practice, Five Elements) or sometimes I need the group communion of a yoga class. Sometimes I need to see a 'bone doctor' – an osteopath or chiropractor – and sometimes I just need to trust my instincts about trying something new and if an opportunity comes up to go for it. Remember, life evolves and creates – don't get stuck in the routines and habits of what you think you should do!

But looking back over the years, the three main legs of what I've done to help keep me balanced have been; one-to-one sessions, yoga classes, and free dance and movement, and those three levels somehow for me mirror life. They comprise being treated, being taught and having free space to express myself. You need someone to intimately share with, you need to have group connection, and you need to move freely! On that note, I actually think we practise yoga to keep us flexible so we can dance – not just dance at classes, clearly, but ultimately to dance with life as we engage with it.

However, here's the crux of it all. In effect, essentially anything can be a therapy or therapeutic experience; it just relies on you being in the right place, at the right time doing the right thing! If it moves your 'energy' in a healing direction, then it's therapeutic! Whether it's a walk in the park, time with a loved one, laughing your head off at a comedy event, or even work, as long as you are making choices that feed and nourish you, it's all good!

This became very evident to me early on. In the year I mentioned in Chapter 4 where I was off work with fatigue after too much time in jobs that burned me out, my body was giving me a massive 'no' to anything stressful whatsoever. But as for going to yoga classes, going out dancing, and all the other therapy work, I thought: bring it on!

I finally went back to work after that year out, but within six weeks I was wrecked again. I remember being curled up on the settee just wondering how I could cope with life and get through it. But eventually the penny dropped when I realised that when I was passionate about something, like during the time off when I'd been doing loads of yoga, dancing and studying about holistic practices, I could see clearly that some activities I was doing were supportive and therapeutic – so naturally I desired them – and other activities were downright injurious to me. But it was only by having so much kindness and so many positive 'therapeutic' experiences that I really got to see this contrast.

Before that I was doing what I now call the 'antidote syndrome' where you have parts of your life that hurt you, and you stay blind to them, and instead try and compensate with other parts. I'll admit that sometimes practical circumstances dictate you have to endure certain things more than you wish – and your soul can see this too. It's life and the variety of experiences helps us grow, but that's not the same as hiding behind these circumstances.

That's the difference. True hardship you live fully in the moment; implied hardship you kind of bring on yourself in some ways as you are scared to live. How many times I've seen in others and myself a sense of restriction because, for example, we convince ourselves we need the income from our present job (that we hate) because it keeps us accustomed to a lifestyle 'we are used to'. Yes, it feels like a kind of hardship as you hate your work, but you have a way out, to step into the soul desire, but you choose not to take it.

One of the big questions in this type of situation that stops people from taking that kind of step, is how much is enough? A lot of my patients refuse to step out from behind a job they hate as they don't feel they have 'enough'. It pains the hell out of me when the patient opposite me tells me that they hate their extremely well-paying job but need to stay in it for another two, three, five years because they like the money and will then enjoy their life 'after' that. That's fine if you are on the breadline, painful if you clearly already have huge resources – which I'm also aware a lot of them have!

The other big question in this type of situation that stops people from changing is not knowing what to move towards, what the soul desires, so you stay rooted to the present spot. Obviously a large part of this book is all about remedying that!

I know it's not sometimes 'the done thing' to jack the job in and do what you actually want to do, but this often comes from a misguided belief instilled into us when we are younger about always wanting more (money, not what your heart desires!), being better, being competitive, and pushing like hell to work your way up the ranks for extra scraps of power and kudos. Ouch.

However, in true hardship, you are following your soul desire, and on that journey things get tough, challenging, but at least you live that hardship fully as circumstances dictate you have to. You might not have enough, and perhaps have to do other work that you might not like, but on some level you feel that the ultimate destination is moving towards harmony and bettering every part of your life so you still feel alive even if some parts of it suck! It's a fine edge, constantly pushing beyond your comfort zone, but ultimately a rewarding one as whenever you choose the path of the soul you choose a more ecstatic and thrilling way of being.

Back to the 'antidote syndrome'. It was as if my mind was thinking, yes I want the best diet ever, yes I want to attend the best yoga class ever, yes I want the best relationship ever, yes I want the best therapies, but for some reason it's okay if I hate my work! Eventually I realised it just made no sense.

Shortly after coming to this understanding I found some flow and positive direction again so my occupation also became an extension of my heart and soul, rather than just acquired skills, and I studied to become an acupuncturist. I've never regretted that movement for one second!

After getting a taste for the enrichment this change brought, this evolution and creativity naturally continued with my training as a yoga teacher and developing many unique classes and events as part of my original Creative Yoga London business. This also just flowed beautifully – when you flow through one door of creation, another naturally appears, and I created a yoga business based on conscious connection, another of my passions!

In my experience I'd always felt a lack of opportunity in the yoga world to connect with the people you'd been in class with, which I always wanted to do as I want to meet people while feeling naturally great, but instead everyone would head home with barely a glance! So with this project I also 'brought the change', as it were, and I created events with a connection ethos like social, singles and couples yoga as well as specialist meditation workshops.

Latterly I have helped facilitate juice detox retreats at the wonderful Moinhos Velhos retreat in Portugal and branched into corporate wellness by having a team working for me teaching in businesses in London. I also do lots of fun stuff like appearing as a wellness expert on an holistic TV channel and giving talks!

So by this point, clearly no more did I need any kind of antidote! No more were parts of my life debilitating; instead the whole landscape was and is enthralling and exhilarating. I don't have to solely 'receive' therapies any more to feel like

I'm engaging in healing energy, as every decision is naturally designed to bring that to my life!

Nuts and Bolts: Tutorial

In this chapter, I'm exploring ways to heal, and I make no apologies that it's longer than the previous chapters as there are so many great things to engage with!

Healing

"In many shamanic societies, if you came to a shaman or medicine man complaining of being disheartened, dispirited, or depressed, they would ask one of four questions.

When did you stop dancing?
When did you stop singing?
When did you stop being enchanted by stories?
When did you stop finding comfort in the sweet territory of silence?
Where we have stopped dancing, singing, being enchanted by stories, or finding comfort in silence is where we have experienced the loss of soul.
Dancing, singing, storytelling, and silence are the four universal healing salves."
Angeles Arrien[16]

I find particular wisdom from this quote as it reminds me that quite simple activities are often things that enable us to thrive, and importantly help to activate our ability to engage with One's soul and 'soul blueprint' (see Chapter 2) in order to keep us feeling clear about our purpose and destiny.

As mentioned above, it's important to note that you don't have to see a therapist to have a therapeutic experience! However because in the modern world we live in such fragmented ways it's also useful to have dedicated practitioners, who we make appointments to see for a concentrated 'dose' of a healing energy, which we will discuss in this section. But it's essential to remember that at its core, all of life is designed to balance.

We actually in effect heal each 'moment', as that's what the intelligence of the universe seeks to do – it's a self-balancing entity – so it could be a visit to someone who practises a healing art or just as equally any activity which enables balance. In flowing with this inherent intelligence we actually heal universal creation itself!
Richard Brook, 2006

Walking into a room full of people laughing, walking through a field of beautiful flowers, being hugged by a loved one, engaging with physical exercise, listening to music – all these things that natural life provides can also all be healing, only we don't always live in tune enough with what we need to stay balanced.

And remember that your body registers every moment you are alive so it all counts! As much as we can seek out concentrated healing experiences, have a look what's happening in your everyday moment-to-moment life. Reflect on the discussion around vibration; everything around you impacts you as it's all made up of vibration – so how is it affecting you? Is it to your taste and energising you? The job you have, where you live, your relationships, they all impact you so have the intention for the highest potential in all areas of your life!

Yoga, mindfulness, meditation and deep relaxation

I'll start with yoga and go deep into its dynamics as it's something that I teach in depth, is such a strong and fundamental aspect of self-care and is amazingly accessible. Essentially, it's a remarkably strong therapy that you apply to yourself, and you can then also apply the wisdom to your entire life.

What is yoga?

Literal meaning of yoga = union

A lot of more westernised yoga nowadays is more aligned to the practice of posture (known as Asana), but in particular in my teaching and practice I work strongly with the awareness of yoga as a state of union, which is what 'yoga' actually translates to.

KEY POINT

Since this state of 'union' is in essence what yoga is, it's essential to work with the idea that yoga is a 'state of being' rather than an achievement of manipulating your body into a particular posture!

This is basic, but the idea that yoga is aligned so fully to posture is so etched into the collective psyche in the Western world that it causes a lot of inhibition! If you go down the route of thinking that yoga is aligned to postural achievement then immediately it limits whether you think you can do it.

Everyone can achieve a yogic state, but not everyone can stand on their head, so whether you can achieve all postures to their fullest extent isn't particularly relevant – how many people on Earth can do that?

There are adaptations to postures that mean that people can work within their own capacities and still achieve a similar effect on the body. This is yoga as this is real life – being in tune with your unique individual qualities and honouring life with expressing them.

There are also masses of scriptures and discussion about the origins of yoga and what it is, but rather than repeat well-trodden ground, this is my perspective:

Yoga is a sense of unity which, through repeated practice on the mat, starts to permeate through your entire being consciously as being your natural state. That feeling becomes transferable as the common denominator across all areas of your life.

The whole of life becomes your yoga practice, dropping things away which don't tie in with that sense of unity. So it starts to permeate all – your social life, your relationships, your work – it all becomes your centre, your 'practice'.

When your whole life becomes your practice, what exactly are we 'practising' for?

It's the sense of unity we feel in our heart, our core, as that aspect of us, some call it soul, is forever unified and part of the light which illumines all. So the yoga practice is ultimately about expanding the perfection of seed soul which exists within and making it as big as possible in your life.

Your life becomes your seed soul expanded; there is nothing excluded from the light that switches on when you do something you love.
What is love? It is the engagement with the prompting of your soul.
Richard Brook, 2015

Yoga 'practice'... practice for what?

Yoga is referred to as a practice, and as the quote above illustrates, the point is that it's actually a practice for what goes on in your life off the mat! What you do, and what you experience on the yoga mat physically, mentally and emotionally, is generally a strong reflection of your physical, mental and emotional patterns off the mat in your life too.

Because your nervous system is more relaxed while practicing your perception begins to turn inwards and you can begin to 'witness' yourself. You can examine and build self-awareness of your body-mind patterns that is invaluable in any situation, and start to choose alternate ways of being. Some general observations you can make:

- Check what's happening in your body; are you comfortable?
- Are you so comfortable you are losing awareness, spacing out and falling into routine?
- Are you pushing yourself too hard?
- Are you listening to the feedback of the body and coming to your senses now in this moment, or are you stuck in the 'idea' in your mind of what you think you 'should' be doing?

Yoga practice also provides opportunities aplenty to look at specific life dynamics. For example, let's take forward bends. You might begin to notice that as you bend your entire focus becomes about how far you can reach, and that striving and pushing forwards leads you to collapse your chest, so you can no longer feel through your heart centre, and your head dips, so you also can't really see where you are going or particularly enjoy the posture either. And this could remind you of how you sometimes push forward like that in life, pushing so hard that you close emotionally, don't enjoy the journey and can't be receptive to what's around you!

Or for example you may be doing a posture where the instruction is to follow your own rhythm or breath, but in reality you lack confidence in tuning into your own flow and timing in a group so consistently keep checking the pace of others around you.

Or the classic is constantly trying to emulate the posture that the teacher or those around us adopt, even if it makes us feel uncomfortable. With the style of yoga that I teach, this can be even more of a challenge as it's about 'feeling' and achieving that state of 'union' rather than how it looks. So the emphasis is about adopting the postures while still feeling whole, finding what's right for you personally despite what others are doing. And this is one of the most important metaphors, because how often does life try and push you into shapes you don't like?

So being able to keep your sense of 'union' and know your own sense of 'centre' and boundaries in light of external forces is a massive skill to have.

Yoga is also fantastic for working with the body-mind experience of your comfort zones. What we often do in our lives is find our initial comfort zones with a situation, and then either stay in it or try and force and push past it, leaving us not fully present in a situation as we have 'left part of ourselves behind' when we pushed out. With yoga, you can find your initial comfort zone, and then relax and open past it, fully present, fully engaged and move past your initial limitations.

For more on yoga as a metaphor for what we do in life, please visit this blog: Yin & Yang in Yoga as Practice for Life[xii]

Yoga styles

Before I progress further, I hasten to add that there are many different types of yoga out there. The experiences I write about are ones which I associate with the 25+ years of practice I've had across a few different styles that I really attune to and open me up – most notably Dru yoga – which has an emphasis on deep relaxation which I find extremely valuable as it takes me into an internal silence and stillness where I engage clearly with my deeper self.

But I've also been in yoga classes that haven't really worked for me and probably wouldn't have the same profound impact. So, if you've never really done yoga consistently before, or have been doing it for a while and it's not really working for you, I'd suggest trying a few different styles, as there are so many out there nowadays. If you go to a class and hate it, don't give up, try another. If the whole experience just feels like a pain fest that you want to space out from, then definitely try another! It can be best to start gentle and work

---

xii   www.creativewellness.co.uk/bookblogs

into harder styles, the point being that like anything else, it has to resonate with you!

I don't think I've ever returned to a yoga class due to a kind of 'discipline'. I never go back because I think 'Oh it's Wednesday at 7pm so I have to go to yoga'. I go back because I can't wait to get there because it feels so good for me. So finding the right class and style can be the difference between the profoundly nourishing experiences I'm about to extol and something that can be relatively non-descript!

I also find that having a relatively gentle yoga like Dru or Hatha as my 'base' regular practice always means it feels sustainable as it can catch and 'hold' me, whatever state I'm in. I love Dru's heart and relaxation focus, as this is what I need.

Harder styles I can maybe go to once or twice, but I just don't feel I can sustain them come rain or shine, as they are too much for my system. At the end of this section I discuss more about various styles of yoga and why you may be more drawn to particular styles depending on your constitution.

For now though, as a brief guide, I've made a list below of some relatively well-known styles of yoga, broadly from most yin (gentle and inward) to most yang (most physically challenging and exertive). Before anyone jumps on my case, it's just a rough breakdown and of course there are many exceptions and variances depending on the teacher's style, etc!

Yoga styles, from most yin (gentle) to most yang (exertive)

Restorative
Dru
Yin

Hatha
Iyengar
Kundalini
Vinyasa flow
Jivamukti
Ashtanga
Power yoga
Hot yoga

What style of yoga is better?

Many years ago, when I first started practising yoga, I may have got into debates about one yoga style being better than another. Fast forward to now and I realise that because different people are constitutionally different (as shown in the section on elements, and also later chakras), naturally they will be drawn to different types of yoga.

As seen in the section on elements, different people have a different proportionality of elements, which relates to the subtle state of internal organs. So people may be drawn to different styles of yoga which stimulate them accordingly. For example, a person with a very strong Wood Element, which associates with ligaments and tendons in the body, may be drawn to a really physically strong yoga like Ashtanga; a person whose main element is Fire, which associates with the heart, may be drawn to a heartfelt yoga like Dru; a person whose main element is Earth, which associates with the muscles, may like a yoga which is a bit softer than Ashtanga but still really stretches them like Hatha or Vinyasa Flow; a person whose main element is Metal, which associates with the lungs, may be drawn to a yoga which involves lots of pranayama and an emphasis on breathing like Kundalini, and a person whose main element is Water, which associates with the kidneys and our ability to deeply rest, may be drawn to a restorative or very slow yoga, like yin yoga.

The 'flexibility' issue and misconceptions

There is massive misconception about yoga and flexibility. Deepening the point above, since yoga is actually about a state of 'being' rather than a posture, how physically flexible you are isn't the ultimate emphasis. Yoga can of course make you more flexible as it involves movements that affect your musculoskeletal structure, but it's much more involved than that.

Compression points

A great deal of a person's flexibility is related to what are known as 'compression points' that are a result of skeletal structure. With all the will in the world, a person may not be able to get the perfect archetype of a posture because the compression points of the bones won't allow them to. Nothing to do with 'flexibility'.

So a person may be moving in accordance with their own physical limitations, and not achieving what the 'perfect' posture is meant to look like, but still achieving the same result – it doesn't matter. Similarly, someone may be particularly flexible, almost hypermobile, but it doesn't make them a yoga expert or mean they achieve ultimate yogic states as they may also have to adopt an alignment that is different from the perfect archetype of the posture in order to get the same benefit.

Absence of tension

For me yoga is much more about the 'absence of tension' as actually being the essence of flexibility. If you think about it, someone could be very flexible and actually wracked with tension, which clearly isn't what we are trying to achieve if we are trying to move towards a state of yogic union. This means moving within your limitations, but in a relaxed fashion. This is the common denominator. I call it intention without tension! It's also important to note, as we'll discuss further later, that tension also consumes a huge amount of energy. So becoming overly tense, either within yoga, as a result of yoga, or in your life generally isn't good for you!

'Stretching' and connective tissue activation

Being an acupuncturist allows me a depth of understanding of what is actually happening within the body physiologically when you engage a posture. As acupuncturists, we work with the understanding of how connective tissue in the body interconnects to the function of organs within the body. So when you enter into a posture it will activate particular fascia and connective tissue which then stimulates the corresponding organs that have a relationship to that connective tissue.

What's important to note here is that if you have an undue amount of tension when you enter into a posture, it can actually inhibit the depth of activation of the connective tissue. So tightly contracting muscles when you enter a posture can to some degree nullify its effect. Relaxing and opening, rather than pushing (which requires tension), can be much more efficacious.

Breathing

Any state of stress or tension in the body inhibits your optimal breathing pattern. This is a bit more of an obvious one. Just watch what happens when you walk into a situation that makes you feel significantly uneasy – you substantially 'hold' your breath. The thing is that stress isn't always this black and white; we are generally under different degrees of stress, and very rarely totally relaxed. Indeed, if we've been under chronic situational stress, even when we are away from that situation the body can take a long time to readjust.

So chances are that even when you think you aren't under stress, your body is still not breathing at its optimal state and yoga can help to make up for this imbalance in a number of ways. Firstly, by alleviating tension from the body and organs it can activate the relaxation response which helps to rebalance the natural breathing cycle. And secondly most forms of yoga will contain some distinct breathing exercises, often referred to as pranayama. Pranayama exercises can very deliberately deepen and lengthen the breath, oxygenating the body in a way which is being compromised when under chronic stress. By using greater lung capacity, they also clear stagnancy out of the lungs and help you feel more vital, vibrant and inspired!

The subtle energetic impact of how you breathe is also worth becoming aware of. When we breathe fully and deeply into our abdomen, it stimulates the lower chakras and gives us a sense of connection to the solidity and security of the Earth underneath us and our body itself. Breathing fully into the middle chakras of our body, our ribcage, enables us to feel aware of what's around us, and breathing fully into our upper chakras connects us to our more subtle thoughts and feelings, essentially our connection to what's above us.

As a human being, to feel whole and balanced we obviously need to inhabit the full spectrum of these faculties, but inhibiting the breath in any of these areas inhibits our experience of them. For example, when we don't breathe fully into our abdomen and lower chakras we can feel disconnected from a sense of being grounded and secure, and when not breathing into our upper chakras and top of the lungs we can lack a sense of inspiration and disconnection from our subtle feelings. So, full spectrum breathing (deep yogic breath as it's often called in practice) can really help to reconnect you to the full essence and potential of being a human being!

It's also worth trying to increase awareness of both your default breathing pattern and also how particular situations tend to influence it – for example if you're a chronic shallow breather you may struggle to feel a sense of security and 'solidity' no matter what the situation is. And you may notice that in certain situations your breath pattern changes significantly, both positively, when you are in a situation that makes you feel comfortable, and negatively, when you are in a situation that generates stress.

Even what is happening with the focus of your attention has an impact on your breathing rhythm. An exercise I teach in my classes is to ask people to quickly observe their breathing pattern, and then see how it alters and relaxes even by placing your attention upon it. See also the following section 'Your Attention has Power'.

How yoga works in achieving a state of 'union'

A great deal of the time, particularly in our Western culture, we can become very aligned to our conceptual mind and intellect (or 'left brain'; see Chapter 5) and become very disconnected from our bodily sensations, creative impulses and the reality of our sensory experience in this moment (right brain). So, in this sense we can see that our default state is often quite an imbalanced one, and we become disconnected from what's around us.

Being at 'One' and stilling the mind

This is where the often-quoted phrase of yoga making us feel more at 'One' comes from. Practice draws you back down into the reality of your body sensations and makes you feel more connected to your environment around you as right brain function is promoted.

As your brainwave patterns shift you change from experiencing yourself as predominantly trains of thought in your mind, and with the activation of the relaxation response you experience a much broader spectrum of reality. You experience being more in the sensory reality of the moment, and being connected to your more subtle thoughts and feelings. This also lends itself to the often-quoted connection to 'body, mind and spirit'.

This shift in brainwave pattern is also responsible for the experience of 'stilling' the mind. Often in our lives our mind is in an overstimulated state, as it's influenced by the nervous system being similarly overstimulated (see Chapter 5) and we are constantly seeking external activities to placate it.

Yoga influences the nervous system from the 'inside out' and changes your state of perception from within which can be quite a profound experience. And repeated practice allows us to build awareness of and change the calibration of our default state from being over-busy to a greater sense of spaciousness without trying to do it by managing the world around us, which is often what we do before realising we have some control over our inner state.

For more on how yoga influences your state via connective tissue please visit this blog: Why Yoga Changes How You Think And Feel - Connective Tissue[xiii]

Your attention has power

Have you ever suddenly turned around to find someone is looking at you and has their attention on you? Or noticed how you feel in a meeting when the attention is on you? No one is physically touching you, yet you can tangibly feel the effect of someone's attention on you. This is because attention – where you choose to place your mind and awareness – has a tangible impact on where it is focused, and it raises the vibration and energises what it is focused on. So when you practice yoga, your attention tends to come 'inside' which subtly nourishes and energises your body. It gives you a vibrant energy field.

Think how much of your average day you spend with your attention focused on things around you, external to you. It's usually a lot, and this can leave us undernourished on a subtle level. When you get subtly depleted like that, you

xiii www.creativewellness.co.uk/bookblogs

can also often end up trying to make up the energy deficit by seeking other people's attention, or from food – basically anything which gives energy. So when you give that attention to yourself when you practice yoga you tend to feel more content, less needy, and you glow!

Fusing yin and yang with yoga and meditation

Following on from the point above regarding placing your attention in the body, this is essentially a fusion of your yin and yang faculties. Your body is the extreme of your yin and your awareness is the extreme of your yang, so by consciously placing your awareness within the body, you are essentially consciously fusing together your yin and yang aspects.

These forces often become separated. We either have our attention turned outwards with only the occasional glimpse of sensation from the body when it 'shouts' loudly enough, or we are unconsciously lost in thought without awareness of our body sensations.

But when yin and yang are consciously fused together it can be a massive creative and transformative force, strong enough to create the seed of new life. Remember the act of conception is the fusion of yin and yang (masculine and feminine) coming together!

To remind yourself about the power of the creative fusion of Yin and Yang please visit this blog: Yin Yang of Awareness - Mind and Matter - The Alchemy of Creation[xiv]

xiv   www.creativewellness.co.uk/bookblogs

'Tuning' into yourself

It's also hugely beneficial to have regular instances where we can 'tune into' ourselves so that we can keep perspective on how our choices in life are affecting us across the spectrum of body, mind and spirit. Having a practice, at least once a week, where you spend quality time with yourself means you can track how you feel in detail from one week to the next and look at what you may have been doing to influence those changes.

You might notice that one week you are substantially tenser than the previous week and notice it's accompanied in your mind with repetitive thoughts about an issue going on around you in life which can be a sign that action may need to be taken, or you need to spend some time integrating the events.

Or maybe one week you find your relaxation much deeper and more peaceful than usual and you can similarly relate it to some changes you have made in your lifestyle. As I have mentioned throughout this book the relaxed state that yoga facilitates enables you to connect to and hear a much deeper part of yourself, the 'quietest voice' inside yourself of your heart and soul.

For more on this please visit this video blog: How Yoga Helps You Hear What's In Your Heart[xv]

So it's a great way to find and get to know your centre, and be aware when you are straying off it!

---

xv   www.creativewellness.co.uk/bookblogs

Focusing on specific postures

People often ask me about whether it's bad practice to repeatedly focus on one particular posture or specific postures that you feel drawn to. Not necessarily!

It's important to remember that the body is always in some posture or another, even when we're sitting down (often slumped) relaxing, standing, or perhaps in the default postures you adopt while at work. So it could well be that the postures you are drawn towards help to counteract the common postures you are adopting in your life – for example, if you work a lot hunched over, you might naturally want to do postures that open your chest.

But nevertheless, these should still be practised alongside a balanced set of postures to help the overall structure achieve its highest potential.

Yoga and superlearning

Have you ever noticed that when you are very busy, you just sometimes can't receive new information? Your brainwave pattern is too amplified to be receptive (basically your mind is too busy!).

Exercises such as yoga co-ordinate both sides of your brain and activate a relaxation response that makes the body and mind much more receptive to new input. When we are faced with a hectic schedule our appetite and time for nourishing ourselves with practices like yoga becomes depleted. So this compromises our capacity to learn.

This ability for yoga to support your ability to learn was identified by education expert Sheila Ostrander who includes it as an integral principle of her 'Super-learning' practices[17].

Please note the reference above to yoga making both the body *and* mind more receptive. This is because we actually learn a great deal through the transmission of energy and information as it hits our body and is absorbed into our chakras and nervous system – and if you are tense or stressed, this is inhibited. We have started to cover phenomenon of the body absorbing vibration and information in the relationships section and will return to it in greater detail later.

For now, think about how we learn much more easily when we are young. Consider that it's because your nervous system is more impressionable and malleable (your 'energy' body is more open) so you more readily absorb information and impressions into your body, creating imprints which shape the nature of the mind. So it would follow that should you once more make the body as malleable, and reopen the energy body, that indeed even as an adult you can reshape and 'change' your mind. This is basically the principle behind 'Super-learning' as discussed above; the mind becomes more receptive to new information again. Basically we are reshaping our interior circuitry and mind landscape with fresh input. We talk more about releasing old patterns and old impressions later (see 'The Impact on Chakras and Your Subtle Vibration').

While there may be a general reduction in how energetically malleable we are when we get older, we are also generally, unfortunately, more closed than we optimally would be due to the difficult conditions of modern life – due to stress and the lack of satisfactory conditions to relax and emotionally engage.

Therefore regular yoga practice, and for that matter other types of therapeutic work, is essential as it consistently works to keep us open, to change and refine what we experience in our mind.

The influence of the teacher

While particular yoga styles do have a similar structure and presentation, there can of course be subtle differences due to the individual teacher. And of course, you might just enjoy a particular teacher's style, personality, vibe, and disposition more than others. There might be something that they particularly express that you feel you can also learn from. For me, I tend to be drawn to teachers with a particularly gentle energy, in whose class I really feel I can relax. I think this is because I actually push myself quite hard in my life, so what balances me is something quite soft!

But equally you might be drawn to teachers with a harder, more rigid or almost sergeant major approach as that might be what you instinctively need to engage with. Trust your impulses, but if you have a negative experience with a particular style of yoga, it can sometimes be worth trying it again with a different teacher in case it was the teacher's style which was wasn't working for you, rather than the style of yoga itself.

The significance of a class setting

The class setting and energetic ambience also has the added dimension of providing essential nourishment to the chakras. As we have seen, the energy radiated from other people helps to feed and nourish us on a subtle level. In the modern world, communal activity is diminished by the strains of modern life and advent of technology, replacing situations where once we may have engaged with other people and benefitted from the energetic exchanges which can take place. In this way yoga supersedes the relative time and space and social and cultural differences of modern life and reconnects us to a common need of all human beings since inception of nourishing our body, mind and spirit.

Deep relaxation

"Relaxation is the KEY to healing! The body cannot heal unless it is relaxed."
Julie Visaka Hotchkiss (Dru Yoga Teacher Trainer)[18]

"Repeated activation of the relaxation response can reverse sustained problems in the body and mend the internal wear and tear brought on by stress."[19]
Relaxation is "a physical state of deep rest that changes the physical and emotional responses to stress" [20].
Dr. Herbert Benson, The Institute for Mind Body Medicine

Immense rebalancing and healing can occur when the body enters into a deeply relaxed state. Renowned yogi and founder of the Art of Living Organisation Sri Sri Ravi Shankar said that 20 minutes of deep relaxation has the same rejuvenation effects as eight hours of sleep[21], but its effects run much deeper than that.

The beautiful state of conscious rest can seem like an emotional makeover at the same time, as the body gives up the stories that it's holding in tension patterns which afflict the system, and as we have discussed earlier it can be a time where discordant vibrational imprints can be released from the body.

I've always found Dru yoga to be immense for achieving an optimal state of relaxation as its heart-warming ambience encourages the body to deeply relax. I used to come back around after a deep relaxation and feel like a new person!

If you have amplified stress in your life, you need amplified relaxation techniques to help to balance you out.

To experience a guided deep relaxation please visit this blog: Need to Chill? Deep Relaxation with Richard Brook[xvi]

Therapeutic subtleties - the impact of discordant energy

The impact on chakras and your subtle vibration

We discussed in Chapter 6 how vibration impacts the body, and can in effect 'rub off on us' – and actually become absorbed into our subtle energetic body. Think about how powerful experiences echo around in you for a while and can also shape your demeanour and expression.

Vibrations enter our body and energy field through the doorway of a chakra, and unless the energy is processed or cleansed the vibrations can soak their way into the tissue and organs – and thus become part of our mind and create repetitive thought patterns.

Practising yoga stretches the soft tissue of the body and via the meridian system stimulates the internal organs, which can enable it to disperse these aggregated vibrations and imprints which can get stuck in the body and energy field.

---

xvi www.creativewellness.co.uk/bookblogs

The aggregation and stagnation is a bit like if you leave a bottle of liquid, such as milk, for a while, and it gathers a layer of sediment, which may become too dense for even the milk underneath to move through and pour out. So it is similarly with vibration in our body: if we don't stretch and move, vibrations gather together and can almost form a layer of crust, density or blocks in our system. Little can get in, or radiate out.

A similar analogy is how air in a space can get stuffy, stagnant and almost become 'dense' when it isn't properly ventilated. So this state of density and stagnation is important to alleviate and avoid, and movement helps with this.

When I'm in a relatively highly energised state such as while I'm dancing or practising acupuncture I can see and sense a shrouded area around a person or chakra, which can be indicative of blockages. Shamanic healers and those who can see a person's subtle 'energy body' also often speak of encrusted chakras or those that are locked down.

Yoga therefore refines us as it stops us getting cluttered up with things that have happened in the past and clears our sensory perception to be more aligned to what is happening in the present moment. As the stagnant energy clears from the organs via the nervous system, it then similarly clears the associated imagery and conceptual language we also experience in the mind. This creates a much more harmonious mind after a class.

Locking the spine

The clearing of discordant energy (as explained above) can also positively influence posture, as the absorption of discordant vibration can also result in us 'locking' the spine, affecting our alignment and structure (essentially we become stiff with tension). This 'locking' happens as we seek to suppress or avoid the feelings we experience through either the external senses from the world around us, or through the internal senses, relating to internally held or generated feelings we don't want to feel.

For an example of how we seek to avoid an external vibration, think of a situation where you spend time around someone who instinctively doesn't feel good to be around. You may start to lock your chest up to protect your heart. This may work in the short term – until you manage to leave the immediate situation – but what happens after prolonged exposure? Your body ends up adopting that position by default.

For an example of how we seek to avoid an internal vibration, imagine you are chronically unsatisfied at work – this could put strain on the liver and gall bladder (which are responsible for creating a plan to keep us growing in life and feeling fulfilled), creating frustration and stagnation in the organs, which for whatever reason we may not want to fully acknowledge, perhaps being fearful of change, and in order to avoid these sensations within the body we similarly 'lock' the spine to avoid the feedback from the organ.

In essence an external discordant vibration can also soon end up becoming an 'internal' discordant vibration if we can't close down quickly enough, as we end up absorbing the vibrations, which can then play havoc with our natural frequencies.

In any of these cases therapeutic support can be helpful to remove any discordant energy and avoid a prolonged period of time holding the structure tight and tense to avoid feeling any of these sensations from outside or inside the body.

Deep relaxation and the release of trauma and vibrational imprints

If we lock vibrations into the body, particularly from trauma, it often means that when the body is triggered, through resonance with the original experience, that we can be 'reminded' of the original experience, and consciously re-experience it.

This can happen at unsolicited, unexpected times when we don't expect it, which can in some situations also be quite traumatic. Essentially we get a 'flashback'. For example, if you have been in a car crash and see a similar car, it can resonate and remind you of the original experience.

These kind of flashbacks can also happen during therapeutic practices when a part of the body-mind is reopened from the state of tension and closure, which then enables the vibration of the original experience that was previously trapped to pass back through the mind. This can happen during bodywork, energywork or even during talk therapies.

In this context, the experience is less of an uncontrolled 'flashback' and more of a controlled 'recapitulation' which enables the trauma from the original experience to be expressed, integrated and alleviated rather than locked into the body. Clearly, the 'flashback' is happening in a much safer environment during a therapeutic session – as long as it's held in the correct manner and the person feels safe to open up.

Within the context of a yoga class, this means having the correct energetic ambience set up in the room for such deep therapeutic work.

However, yoga can also sometimes provide the right condition for traumas to be released without the need for them to be re-experienced on the conscious level. This is because after practice, the deep relaxation that people experience at the end of the class can take the person into the most deeply relaxed brainwave pattern of delta waves, but of course the body is still feeling the opening and releasing effects of the yoga. This means that the releasing process is going on while the person is very deeply relaxed.

Meditation and chakra clearing

As well as being a fantastic inner awareness tool to give us insight into what is happening in our body-mind, meditation also promotes chakra clearing and balancing.

Meditation opens chakras which then allows discordant vibrations to be cleared from the system, bringing a greater sense of peace and wellbeing. Sitting with a relatively upright spine also allows the more subtle vibrations of the upper centres to rebalance with the lower ones, as the posture enables a clearer energy flow up and down the spine and therefore between all seven centres, as opposed to in everyday life activities where areas of the body and the spine can contract or be affected by what we are doing.

The significance of sensitivity

A significant point around absorbing discordant energy and

locking the spine is in relation to our external senses, and this is that it can depend to some degree on how sensitive we are.

Some people are naturally more 'thick skinned' than others, feeling less sensitive to the world around them. You could line up 50 people in front of a discordant energy source, and those with a much greater degree of sensitivity could feel much more afflicted than others, and become more locked down and tense.

Some people are just naturally more sensitive, myself included as I've mentioned already, and in some environments like the holistic world it's a strength, but when I used to work in highly discordant environments it was often perceived by those around me as a weakness.

In the instance of high sensitivity, it can be worth exploring therapies (such as acupuncture) which may balance excessive sensitivity, as far as nature will allow, but past that point it may just be a case of interpreting your sensitivity as a navigational aid for your health and life purpose – that it will guide you towards things that help you thrive, and stay clear of things that aren't congruent for you.

It's also worth noting that sensitive people can sometimes choose to 'body armour' to avoid feeling – putting on extra weight or bulking up muscle through exercise to make them less susceptible to external input, albeit that these approaches can evidently lead to other levels of imbalance.

Exercise: Yoga

1. Try yoga!
If you are a beginner, try three different yoga classes – remember there are lots of different styles and if you just do one and don't like it, it can limit your perception!

2. 'Life yoga' check list

Yoga is a practice for what we are doing in our daily life, and we are aiming to bring the same awareness into our life off the mat as we have on it.

So just like you would in a yoga posture in a class, observe the following points as often as you can for a week. Try and observe these points during different activities that you do. You can think of different activities you do in your life just like different postures in the class – some are more challenging than others! For example, observe yourself at work, in various relationships, while relaxing, while exercising and so on. Reinforce the analogy that in life off the mat, just like in a class, you are always in some form of posture:

- Be aware and mindful; check what's happening in your body.
- Are you comfortable?
- Are you so comfortable you are losing awareness, spacing out and falling into routine and energy stagnation?
- Do you need to invigorate your awareness and open a little further beyond your comfort zone?
- Are you pushing yourself too hard?
- Are you overly comparing yourself with people around you or focusing on what feels right for you?
- Are you listening to the feedback of the body – coming to your senses now – or just the 'idea' of how things 'should' be in your mind?

For more on chakra dynamics please visit: Chakras: Your Body Your Mind by Richard Brook[xvii]

---

xvii www.creativewellness.co.uk/bookblogs

To experience Dru yoga please view the videos here: Yoga with Richard Brook[xviii]

Mindfulness and meditation

There is a great deal of debate about the exact individual definitions of mindfulness and meditation, let alone the subtle distinctions between them. So those who are deep into yogic philosophy could probably spend a while dissecting the semantics of what I write here, however my writing is based not only on many years of my own practices, but also generally in alignment with what you may find from many other sources. And of course, it's not about the concept, semantics and subtle distinctions; as ever, it's about the practices and what may be true for you. Try them and then share your truth.

Overview

Mindfulness and meditation, and the distinction between them, could be defined in the following way:

Mindfulness – Awareness and observation of 'what is'
Meditation – A technique which moves the mind towards a
    transcended state, towards stillness

There are many different styles of meditation out there. Traditionally we tend to think of the sitting still, cross-legged image, but you can get moving meditations – such as with 5Rhythms Dance, sound meditations, walking meditations; the list goes on!

---

xviii www.creativewellness.co.uk/bookblogs

Indeed Indian mystic Osho's *The Book of Secrets* is a commentary on 112 different meditation techniques presented in the ancient Hindu text the *Vijnana Bhairava Tantra*[22]. So there is a broad spectrum of practices to consider when it comes to trying to create clear definitions! Lots of shades of grey!

Looking now at mindfulness, for me it's something which you can practice at any time, in any place. As it relates to the observation of what is, right now in this present moment, it is applicable at any time. You can be mindful right now of the sensation of air against your face, the tingling sensation in the sole of your foot, the feel of the clothing against your abdomen, the sound of the birds or the flickering of a candle in front of you. And you can be mindful walking down the stairs, driving your car down the motorway or washing the dishes. Mindful while crossing the road or mindful while quickly picking up broken glass while the neighbours' music blasts through the walls, rattling your sideboard.

And mindfulness is also one of the constituent aspects of meditation, as while practising a meditation you have to be mindful of what you are doing, of course.

However, the two aren't necessarily interchangeable. As noted above in the definition of the practices, meditation is more of a practice which for me actually transcends the regular functions of the mind while mindfulness, in some cases, tends to engage them.

So while mindfulness engages the mind, awareness and senses, meditation uses mindfulness as one of its foundations, but in order to actually initiate a process which starts to take you quite significantly beyond its regular state of functioning.

Let's return to our earlier example of being mindful while

quickly picking up broken glass while your neighbours' music is blasting through the wall rattling your sideboard. Yes, you can be mindful while this is happening, but is this particularly conducive to a deeply meditative state? Not really.

Or people often give the example of driving a car as being meditative. Yes, to some degree it relaxes the mind, and yes you have to be mindful while driving, but could you really be deeply meditating while heading around the M25 at 70mph? Deeply mindful, yes, but in a deep transcended state of meditation? No, because you can't withdraw your senses deep enough while still having some 'outward' focus.

So mindfulness can get you so far, but meditation takes you further.

Key ingredients to meditation practice

Internal awareness

So what are some of the key ingredients that make the difference between mindfulness and meditation? Internal awareness is one of the keys. Picking up the glass off the floor engages your external senses, but doesn't necessarily engage your self-awareness, whereas being acutely aware of your own thoughts, feelings and sensations while picking up the glass adds in an extra layer and creates a link between the inner and outer world and a sense of 'wholeness'.

Supportive environment

However, those situations of the broken glass, blasting music, and driving still pull a huge amount on your external senses, and likely wouldn't allow for the internal awareness and withdrawing of the external senses that deep meditation requires.

There is a reason that meditation often happens in relatively cordial, silent environments (or at least has an element of this during the practice), as this is more conducive to allowing the senses to relax. Even meditations that include a very active element such as some of Osho's also have a silent phase (we'll discuss some of the reasons for a more active element to meditation later).

So generally, in order to move into a fuller state of deep meditation, you'd need to drop the external focus that is being demanded of your senses by discordant situations, as it can stop the mind from getting past a certain point.

In Western culture we are prone to overstimulation due to the demands of our lifestyles, and this forces our attention outward more than the natural flow would. As we discussed in Chapter 4, this strains both the organs responsible for our alertness and also doesn't allow sufficient time and conditions for energy to return to the interior of the body and allow the body and organs to deeply rest and replenish.

This creates what we often call the monkey mind, where your attention is in a pattern of 'jumping around'. So when you reduce the amount of outward stimulation, it can allow a much higher quality and concentration of energy to return to the interior of the body, and promote a much more harmonious body and therefore mind.

Discipline

Another key ingredient of a meditation practice is that there has to be discipline, or focus, as it's the application and commitment to the technique which makes the difference.

This might sound like a basic statement, but it's very important.

Meditation challenges you because of what you find 'inside' and often we don't apply the dedication required to make a technique as effective as it could be, as what we experience internally can feel uncomfortable, at least at first. No matter what technique you are using, as long as you are consciously alert (as in not asleep – another key ingredient!) you have the choice to continually reapply yourself to the technique.

As we discussed in Chapter 5, the mind moves between phases of alertness and drifting around, and each time you come to an alert phase you must reapply your focus to the technique, which is where the efficacy is. This will facilitate the changes in alignment with the particular style of meditation you are doing, whether it's influencing your brainwave pattern, subtle energy body or a different mechanism, unique to the practice you are doing.

How meditation works

With so many different types of meditation, it's a little tricky to generalise or break down individual practices in great detail, particularly as we've identified that it's not necessarily what someone is just doing with their body, but rather there are certain internal ingredients of self-awareness and discipline to the technique alongside having the correct environment. However, we can summarise to a degree.

With a body-centred meditation practice (i.e. one which involves a degree of self-awareness of the body, breath, feelings and sensation) the application of the technique will begin to change your brainwave pattern and awareness away from the aspect of the mind which we often get 'lost' in and believe to be who we are, which is more related to our 'intellect'. On a rudimentary level, we will refer to this aspect of us as our 'left brain'.

What the continued application of the technique does, and the continued awareness of the body, breath, feelings and sensation, is start to amplify right brain function – which is a much broader aspect of our self connected to a much greater field of awareness. This shift in focus has a few effects. Firstly, it is very soothing to the nervous system and begins to calm down a sense of discordance that can exist within.

Secondly, as the nervous system relaxes it has the effect of 'quieting' the mind, in effect pulling your mind away from the cycle of creating more and more conception and thought that happens via the left brain, and gradually wrestling the default state of perception to a more balanced state between left and right brain.

However, the mind will continually fluctuate between left and right brain when you are practising so it's absolutely essential, in order to create the change in brain wave pattern that comes with amplified right brain function, that you keep your discipline and focus on the technique (see 'Discipline' above). Essentially you must focus on body, breath and senses when you come to points of conscious alertness, otherwise you just get lost in your left brain intellect again.

This is sometimes easier said than done, as we like our thoughts, intellect and 'ego' voices and they don't like to let go, so have the courage to persevere, otherwise you will go nowhere!

Practice also moves us closer to our sensory intelligence,

so we change our experience of the subtle feelings within us. Thus when we receive the subtle guidance of the heart and soul we don't experience it as clunky conceptual language in the mind which struggles to do justice to what we are actually feeling, but instead simply experience it more as a sense of intuitive knowing and feeling.

It also begins to change the 'seat' of our consciousness from the vantage point of the conceptual mind to that of the soul, and if you persevere with your practice enough – persevere generally and in each particular session – you may actually break through entirely to soul consciousness altogether. Remember your soul voice within is a seed or 'extension' from a much greater source, so with continued practice you get used to moving up and down this spectrum of consciousness.

Some days you may well be stuck on the level of the conceptual mind with lots of left brain function, lots of inner chatter, and other times you might start to climb the ladder and the thoughts start to drop away somewhat and you feel the promptings and nourishment of your heart and soul within (remember the soul sits in the heart) – a sense of 'lightening up'; and other days you might ascend right to the top of the spectrum where all internal voices start to drop away and you start to not only feel the promptings and light of the soul seed within, but actually ascend even higher and have an even more direct experience of the soul source, which is otherwise known as a sense of enlightenment!

When I really 'hit the light' when meditating (which would be where I have moved my perception up the consciousness spectrum towards 'source' or 'soul') for the most part my external awareness is withdrawn and it's as if I'm internally coming over the crest of a hill into sunshine while feeling totally relaxed and the light obliterates virtually all of the thoughts in my mind. I feel a sense of inner calm and perhaps just the voice or essence of my soul.

I'm not really one who thinks that this is a linear process, that each time you meditate the mind gets clearer and closer to source, but rather we move up and down a spectrum, depending on what's going on in our lives etc.

KEY POINT

Meditation and having a still mind are two separate things.

Remember, meditation is a process or technique that moves you towards that still mind. You have to do the journey. Sometimes there is a lot of traffic on the way! Sometimes there is traffic the entire way!

But the point is you're still meditating; it just doesn't necessarily equate to always having a 'still mind'.

The most common thing that people say to me when I bring up the subject of meditation is that they can't do it, as their mind is always busy. This is a huge issue, as you can be meditating hard, with all the key ingredients and right technique but the mind can still be busy. It doesn't mean you aren't doing the process (which in the best of cases can be gradual in any case), it just means at that given time that your mind is busy, which can happen even as an experienced meditator.

As we have explored, the amount of internal chatter in your mind is linked to the activity in your nervous system. You could have a person who has been meditating every day for 30 years, but give them a particularly chaotic and stressful day and when they sit to meditate then there could still be a massive amount of internal chatter. The chatter may be at a more reduced volume and density than someone who's never meditated before, since it stands a good chance that with such a practice history the nervous system has a more underlying state of calm than most, but it could still be there.

And you could take a person who has never meditated in their life, and if their nervous system is particularly calm when they sit down to practise they could have as still a mind as anyone, ever!

Take away stress and distress and replace with calm, peace and nourishment around you and a sense of being on the correct path in life and the mind is naturally calmer. The catch 22 is that you often need to go inside and meditate to listen to the subtle energies inside of you in order to get closer to what you are meant to be doing in life to make the choices that bring the calm!

Perspective and self-awareness

Regular meditation helps you generate perspective and its very close ally, wisdom. Similarly to yoga, when you meditate regularly you begin to be able to track your internal state and then start to build a 'back catalogue' and internal awareness of how you are and therefore what might be contributing to your state. This will enable you to make wise choices to keep the balance.

And the inner peace can become somewhat addictive. If you are used to having a stiller mind and suddenly you find yourself in distress, it can feel much more unwelcome and you can be keener to sort it out. On a macro level, it can also tell a story in itself if you go through a phase of not wanting to meditate at all – not just about what the contents of the mind are in detail, but just the very fact you do not want to sit with yourself in the broader sense.

We often become addicted to external stimulus to drown out our internal voices. Just look around at people and the amount of constant distraction people choose to escape the voices in their own head.

Once you start tuning inwards and using meditation techniques you soon start to shift your default calibration point towards embracing internal awareness, becoming more at ease with it, and then being able to catch yourself when you are seeking to avoid it – choosing to distract yourself. And being conscious when you are doing this in itself tells you something! What don't you want to hear or take action in your life about?

I used to have this pattern highlighted to me through my practice of 5Rhythms Dance. This was a practice I would do at least weekly, often more, and was a way for me to connect deeply with my inner self.

The occasions when I wouldn't want to go and dance I knew there was something I didn't want to face in my life, as I wasn't wanting to face the inner awareness and prompting I would experience within when I danced. Several times before changing jobs in particular – when I've been scared to make the decision that I have to leave – I'd stop dancing for lengthy periods, but the fact I didn't want to dance, to move, was of course totally representative of the fact that the energy wasn't flowing any more.

Energy wasn't flowing through me from 'outside' and therefore also wasn't moving 'within' me. Or more poetically, you could say I wasn't in a good position between Heaven and Earth and living out my inspiration and guidance from the collective consciousness and manifesting it, so I was stuck in my life, stuck in my body, and then also of course stuck in my mind.

The cumulative impact

While we have noted that meditation isn't necessarily a linear path towards enlightenment, evidently the more you meditate, the greater amount of 'light' you begin to 'let in' and get used to experiencing, and it does start to have a cumulative effect on your system.

This is because it starts to clear away the discordance within the system that can 'clutter' you up internally. So you are more likely to have experiences of enlightenment, and feel comfortable with it the more you practice. I say 'comfortable' for a very good reason – if you are used to experiencing yourself as a constant stream of thoughts within, it can be a bit thought provoking, to put it mildly, when you start to change your vantage point and experience of self away from that conceptual mind, more towards the heart and soul.

Personally, because I watch my inner world so intently, I can see when I'm starting to fall down the spectrum towards the inner dialogue taking over, and then I'll do some kind of practice to bring some light back through and 'raise my vibration'. A bit like topping up on 'light' which helps to dispel the heaviness and discordance of repetitive thoughts.

It has a similar impact whenever you are doing something soulful (when your soul is really fully in your body) – the light of that soulful embodiment disperses heavy errant energies and thoughts which can bog you down. Here it's the practice of meditation that is allowing the soul energy to increase within the body, and gives the chance to turn on a tap or reservoir to continually top it up!

Another way of looking at the dynamic impact of meditation is that, like soul embodiment, it essentially puts your heart back in charge. Since the soul seed sits in the heart, when you meditate (which connects with soul) it amplifies your heart energy, which brings us full circle to our earlier discussion that when the heart is in charge, the other organs feel secure and relax. This awareness of the primacy of the heart is a key facet of Chinese medicine where the heart is the supreme controller, and in Dru yoga. Follow your heart, only make sure you can hear it! And meditation lets you hear it as it calms down the other organs, and lets it speak louder at the same time!

Different types of meditation practice

There are lots of different meditation styles across a broad, broad spectrum! You would be surprised as to what could fall into the category, but it's partly because, as we've identified, it's not necessarily about a particular act or action with the body, but it's more defined by several key ingredients. For example, two people could be sitting in silence side by side; they both 'look' the same, but one could just be well, sitting, and the other could be in a meditative process as they are actively engaging in a self-awareness technique.

As mentioned earlier, Osho wrote a book detailing 112 different techniques! And it's not just that they have a subtle variance between them; some actually involve shouting, screaming, jumping, laughing and crying. So again, it's not just about the external expression of the action, but more about the state of awareness.

The more 'active' meditations can be beneficial for a number of reasons. As I've been outlining, the activity in the mind is linked to the activity in the nervous system, so if you combine your meditation practice with some activities which balance the nervous system then the mind will be clearer. Staying with the Osho themed meditations, the shouting, jumping, etc., are all ways to balance the organs in the body and remove emotional suppression and stagnation which play havoc with the nervous system and create a very discordant mind space.

So by combining the more active aspect of the practice, with self-awareness, you are raising your vibration[23] (as your attention is within your body – see 'Your Attention Has Power' earlier in this chapter) and clearing energy blocks and obstructions within the physical body which calms the nervous system. Thus when you arrive at the more 'still' aspect of the meditation practice your mind is much clearer!

It's worth noting that even the more dynamic styles of meditation do generally have a more 'still' section, as the dynamic parts are there to prepare the ground for the still part that comes after. In essence, this is also what practising yoga before meditation achieves (yoga is often referred to as a preparation for meditation) as it also calms the nervous system and soothes the internal organs so that the subsequent meditation is of a clearer quality.

It's also what we all do to some degree, even in our daily life. How often have you felt or said that you need to go for a walk to help 'clear your mind'? What you are doing there is no different – you're doing activity to help balance your nervous system so that your mind is clearer and you can 'think straight'!

This is why I also particularly enjoy practices like 5Rhythms Dance and Movement Medicine. The movement of the practice relaxes the body and soothes the organs so by the time you end the practice in the rhythm of 'stillness' you feel much clearer.

So at different times it's possible to favour different styles of meditation depending on how you are feeling. Sometimes if you are internally very busy then a movement-based practice can be useful, but if you are feeling super zen then you may wish to do the sitting still styles. Even different seasons might create a preference – in the spring, when there is naturally more uprising energy around, I tend to favour meditations that involve movement, and in the winter, when the rhythm of nature is accordingly slower, I can then tend to sit still for longer!

The influence of your culture

We often have a somewhat idyllic picture of what we think meditation practice should look like. For example, the images abound of a person sitting cross-legged yogi style by the side of a tranquil lake or atop a mountain, and if we can't do that then we somehow feel we are deficient. I think this can also be a prevalent perspective in the yoga world, comparing what we do in practice now to what might have been the cultural norm in India where the practice originated. But the reality is we don't live under the same circumstances. The cultural conditions, stresses and strains are hugely different in the Western world, allied with a lack of meaningful human connection too.

This can mean that our nervous systems are in a vastly different state and need more active style meditations which help to flush and move the emotions around first before we can sit down and be calm.

To experience a simple meditation process, please visit this blog: Meditate With Me[xix]

What happens when you meditate or tune into a healing energy

Image 10 (see page 247) represents what happens in our chakra system when we apply a healing force to our being, whether that's through meditation or other means. You might like to revisit Chapter 3 for a chart showing the various associations of the chakras, as this gives us an idea of what faculties become compromised when our chakra system is off balance. For example, if you absorb discordant thought level energy into your third eye it will affect your perception, just like absorbing discordant energy into your solar plexus chakra can affect your digestion.

However, it's important to note that our chakra system is just one layer of the many systems in the body that interrelate. So, for example, even applying a healing force to the organs via the meridian system (through acupuncture for example) would still afford a change in the chakra system too, as what expresses through the chakra system is connected to the organs and meridian system – and vice versa.

---

xix www.creativewellness.co.uk/bookblogs

In the top of the image, we see an archetypal representation of the chakra system in its optimal state. Basically all chakras are operating at optimal frequency, which means they are free of as much outer 'debris' as possible, and also the underlying physiology is also as stress free as possible.

Outer 'debris' refers to cluttered vibrational energy from the environment around us that 'sticks' to our energy body – such as from other people or the place itself. Think about when you've spent time with someone and you walk away with a sense of their 'voice' or emotional intonation still with you, or you have been in a place and leave still 'buzzing' or 'drained' with its energy – like you are carrying it with you.

As regards the underlying physiology, when organs are stressed, toxic, or in distress this also reflects through the chakra system.

The double-ended arrow to the left side of the image shows that a person's perceptual 'reality' is balanced between the chakras, that their consciousness spans equally from a sense of connection to the Earth, through to a sense of clear connection with what's around them, and the space above. All human faculties are clearly represented and balanced in that person's experience of life. Please note, although they are not necessarily recognised states of illness in a Western sense there are often subtle imbalances where we may, even in the best of circumstances, feel less connected to the Earth (being grounded) or what's around us or what's above us (connection to the collective consciousness and sense of life 'inspiration'). It's also important to remember that in reality we often carry all kinds of subtle debris and vibrations in our chakras – it's part of who we are, but we want to avoid placing as much further strain on them as possible!

Chakras in stress and imbalance

Moving clockwise, the next illustration shows what starts to happen when we apply stress factors. Chakras become distorted, can start to draw to a close (narrowing of the aperture as the nerves that form the basis of the chakra begin to contract), or actually can become frazzled from too much discordant vibrational activity. This also then reflects in the radiance of the chakra around the body – the energy field becomes 'dulled'. There are lots of things that can contribute to this happening, both from outside and inside the body. For example, if you spend a great deal of time in environments where people think in heavily distorted ways, these thought-forms and the vibration of them hang in the air (literally) and can start to clog your upper chakras, with your mind also picking up some of the vibrations of those thoughts.

Too much time on computers, phones, laptops and exposure to Wi-Fi can distort your third eye chakra in particular, frazzling its subtle frequency and affecting the clarity of your perception. Not feeling comfortable to speak your truth can inhibit the throat; aggressive or discordant environments can particularly contract the heart chakra, and for that matter any of the others as they feel repudiated by discordant environments. The solar plexus chakra can also take a battering when we aren't expressing and asserting ourselves properly, the sacral chakra contracts when we don't feel comfortable 'in our belly' with our surroundings or people we are with (things going on around us that we struggle to 'digest'), and the base chakra gets really out of whack similarly if we are standing on ground that feels shaky, when we are in fear, and just when we are actually standing on Earth that is similarly off its natural frequency. This is actually usually the case in most urban environments when we are standing on concrete, usually with many electrical cables underneath and other vibrations that are foreign to the body!

And then of course we have the more internally generated chakra distorters, which distress the organs and reflect in the chakras. Factors involved in this can be, for example, poor diet and excessive alcohol consumption, substances we may take (prescribed and unprescribed), lack of exercise and emotional expression.

As we can also see, the arrow at the right hand side indicates the gravitational direction of consciousness is down. This means the person's vibration is becoming denser and 'heavier' ('heavy vibes, brother!') than what is optimal.

The person may be cut off, or have a sense of being cut off from the life spring of energy that is the source of light behind all creation. Spiritual ideas may feel like non-sense as with little or no connection to the greater consciousness above there is little in the way of expansive awareness to relate to. It can also be a feature of this state of denser vibration that we do also become overtly more focused on the material world around us – to make up for the loss of subtle satisfaction and energy from connection to source. So there can be an overemphasis on consumption and possession, and a sense of scarcity that can be observed through relationships with food, material goods, relationships and wealth.

However, in another respect the direction of the arrow is notional; it doesn't necessarily mean the person is cut off from the collective consciousness or space above, more that they are in negative trajectory and the overall vibration is becoming heavy. So for example, a person could be ungrounded, have their 'head in the clouds', and still actually have this sense of density about them.

So the picture isn't good!

Chakras in healing

Continuing clockwise, the third illustration in Image 10 shows what happens when we 'heal'.

When we heal, we open up to allow a higher vibration to pass through our being to recreate balance. It's important to note here that although the illustrations also show a person in what could be considered a typical meditation pose, there are many ways of raising one's frequency to come back to balance. Yes, meditation is very much one of them – you basically open and allow a pouring forth of energy into your body – but this can also be achieved through any number of other means too! Dance and movement, art, singing, yoga, hugging, talking (especially if speaking the truth), jumping around the room, basically whatever works for you to reconnect back to 'source'.

In this circumstance we aren't trying to heal through consumption (one of the perils we pointed out from the previous illustration is that when you are in an imbalanced state you tend to want to make up the shortfall in energy by consuming) but rather plugging into something much greater than the ego mind at all.

This also applies to the relationship dynamic with anyone who is assisting you in 'healing' – a practitioner, for example, who isn't trying to artificially boost you with their own energy, but rather to get you back on track yourself. What happens is that we receive a high vibration energy into our energy body, which the third illustration shows, which begins to clear stagnancy, discordance and density out of the chakra system and person's auric field.

Also conducive to this clearing process is being in environments that are clear and away from heavily polluted or toxic thought forms (somewhere that you feel you can 'think' clearly) that clog your mind, and similarly somewhere that you feel physically comfortable, that your chakras aren't trying to shy away from or 'close' from. Being out in nature is perfect for this, as the micro-vibration that is present in natural living matter resonates harmoniously with that of the body itself, so it feels no need to contract and close.

As you can see, at the epicentre of each chakra is a high frequency speck of light, which is a high vibration energy that helps the chakra to rebalance back towards optimal. You could liken this process, metaphorically, to the idea that while chakras span the entire colour spectrum, white light contains within it all wavelengths of visible light. So rather than just targeting the frequency of a specific chakra, when you open to this greater vibrational 'white light' energy it actually feeds, nourishes and corrects the imbalances throughout all chakras.

As we can also see, the directional arrow points upwards, to represent that the direction of consciousness is up. Again, this is a notional direction, not to be confused with becoming ungrounded, more that the raising of consciousness (which can actually make you feel more present within your body) helps to correct us if we have become too 'earthbound', too dense, and it is just bringing your energy back to optimal balance across all human faculties.

Incidentally, the first name that I gave to my holistic wellness business? White Light Unlimited!

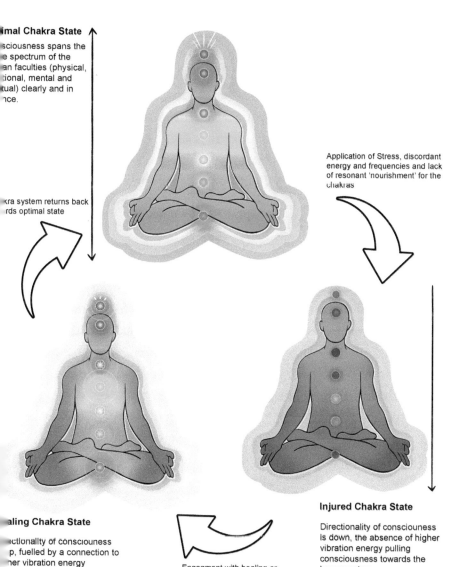

imal Chakra State

sciousness spans the
e spectrum of the
an faculties (physical,
ional, mental and
tual) clearly and in
nce.

kra system returns back
rds optimal state

Application of Stress, discordant
energy and frequencies and lack
of resonant 'nourishment' for the
chakras

Injured Chakra State

Directionality of consciousness
is down, the absence of higher
vibration energy pulling
consciousness towards the
lower centres.

Engagment with healing or
therapeutic activity or therapy

aling Chakra State

ctionality of consciouness
p, fuelled by a connection to
her vibration energy

Image 10: What happens when you heal - from the chakra
perspective

Copyright Richard Brook 2018

247

Exercise: Meditation

Sit and focus your attention approximately two finger widths beneath your navel, and if your sensory acuity allows, two finger widths behind your navel, towards the centre of your body (so your attention ideally is slightly inside your body – if this isn't possible placing your attention on the surface of the body is fine too). This area is known in Chinese medicine as your Sea of Qi, and focusing your mind here can further amplify its energetic potency.

Sit and observe this point for 20 minutes. Sit comfortably but with your spine as straight as you can. Visualise your sitting bones anchoring down into the Earth and the top of your head growing up towards the Sun above.

Don't forget one of the lessons learned earlier in the book around the patterns of the mind: observe that the mind naturally flows between awareness and drifting around in 'thought'. This is the natural action of the mind and don't give yourself a hard time for getting lost in thought.

But each time you become consciously aware again, diligently reapply the technique. Very little will happen unless you reapply the technique.

For one week, try doing this meditation at different times. Sometimes meditate in the morning, sometimes the evening. Do it sometimes after exercise, sometimes when you feel happy, sometimes when you feel stressed. Afterwards make a note of how busy the mind was – score it from 1 (very quiet) to 5 (totally busy).

See if you can notice any patterns. It's not about trying to be perfect, but more building self-awareness and getting to know how your mind works. For example, you might find that your mind is much quieter after exercise, or in the mornings, or after a hug with a loved one, but again, the point is, you are still meditating no matter how busy it is. You are just building awareness of what happens in your mind depending on the activity in your nervous system and starting to track when your mind might be calmer and building your inner knowledge of that.

To experience a guided 'unity meditation' please visit this blog: Unity Meditation[xx]

Acupuncture

There are plenty of references in this book which relay the potency of acupuncture, both in the wisdom of its philosophy and practical therapeutic efficacy. The fact that it places human health in the broad context which includes our relationships with the natural world around us, occupations, personal relationships and the need to follow our own path and life purpose, means it's a system of health which has the capacity to take into account every nuance of your life and understand it's within your instincts to thrive.

Focusing on the physical level, it works wonders in alleviating deeply held tension from the body. So it can be particularly useful if someone has a structural issue in the body which, although it appears on the surface is originating from the superficial fascia (such as muscles), is actually happening due to what we think of as 'stagnation' of energy within the organs, which then has a knock-on effect to disturb the structure.

---

xx   www.creativewellness.co.uk/bookblogs

Balancing first at this very deep level enables greater capacity for the structural levels – muscles, ligaments, tendons and skeletal alignment – to also then rebalance too. So in some cases, a combination of this deep constitutional treatment alongside more distinct fascia-based treatments – massage, physiotherapy, etc. – can be a very effective combination. As can acupuncture alongside chiropractic or osteopathy for similar reasons – it can be easier to manipulate and adjust the skeletal structure after acupuncture treatment as tension has been alleviated.

In Chinese medicine, there is essentially no separation between body, emotions, mind and spirit, so it's possible to treat emotional, mental or 'spirit' level imbalances through the meridian system of the body. Meridians correspond through the entire spectrum of our physical, mental, emotional and spiritual health, and upon identifying the need, treatment can effect profound change on any of these levels. That being said, like all practices, there are distinctions between various acupuncture styles and the individual focus of the practitioner. The style I practice, Five Elements, is perhaps more widely associated with encompassing the more subtle levels of the human being, with the other main style, Traditional Chinese Medicine (TCM), arguably more clinically focused, so it's good to do some research to see what style suits you best!

Bodywork

There are many bodywork practices that work more distinctly with soft tissue, from deep tissue massage to more subtle modalities such as cranio-sacral therapy where the practitioner may have relatively stationary hands on specific points on the body. All of these can be tremendously beneficial if it's the right therapy for you, at the right time. The changes in the physical body then influence the energy body.

Energywork

'Energy'-based practices, such as 'energy healing' or the more well-known practice of reiki, are even more subtle modalities of healing. These practices may involve little or no touch on the physical body and work by the practitioner channelling various frequencies through their hands into the recipient's electromagnetic (energy) field. These changes in the energy body then influence a change through the various denser layers of the being all the way through to the physical.

All efficacious therapeutic modalities will affect a change in the chakra system of the recipient, as outlined earlier in the chapter (please see image 10: what happens when you heal – from the chakra perspective). However, it's fair to say that some therapies work a little more from the 'inside out' by affecting a change in the deeply physical layers of the body which then reflect through the 'energy body' and chakra system, but others work from the 'outside in' where adjustments in the subtle layers on the body then influence the more physical layers of the being. Energywork works more so on this basis, assisting in clearing chakras that are clogged or distorted.

It may also be helpful to have more than one therapy – either physical or energetic – within your awareness that you can reach out to, depending on what your need is at any one time. I would hasten to add, though, that combining courses of treatments simultaneously doesn't always work so well, and it's best to consult with the practitioners involved on that matter!

Dance and movement

Free dancing or movement practices which similarly facilitate a person into a space of spontaneous expression can create huge therapeutic shifts. Not only do they move the spine with the many benefits of stimulating internal organs but they help to disperse tension from the soft tissue, free up areas of constriction in the body (thus the mind) and also allow for a clearing and cleansing on the subtle mental and emotional levels as they also remove stagnancy from our subtle 'energy' and stimulate the chakra system.

Practices I'd thoroughly recommend are 5Rhythms Dance, Movement Medicine or Authentic Movement, however the crucial point is that the practice facilitates a sense of ease in you to move and relax. Your local nightclub can be fun, and it certainly has its plus points, but it might not feel quite as harmonious to your precious heart vibration and encourage it to open, or support the clarity of your third eye, with so much consciousness distortion around you through alcohol, as is often the case.

The beauty of a practice such as 5Rhythms is that, like the Five Elements system, it recognises that we have a spectrum of elements which encompass our being, and therefore plays music which covers this spectrum, allowing all aspects of us to be met and moved. Each rhythm and area of the spine resonates on a different frequency, so attending a 5Rhythms class enables each area of the spine, each chakra, to be exposed to the vibrations, which allow it to open.

Dancing – putting your body and instincts back in charge

Throughout the day we are frequently subconsciously engaging with body behaviour which brings balance: after a while in front of a computer you may find yourself stretching, when you get tired eyes you may find yourself pressing an acupuncture point in the corner of the eyes, and after a nervous or stressful encounter we may press points in our palms which bring balance.

So the body has its own intelligence to enable it to unravel tension and balance, however we don't often allow enough time or space for this process to balance against the amount of strain we experience in modern life. Allowing the whole body free space for it to move gives it much more opportunity to balance as a whole, rather than just individual parts.

Before I qualified as an acupuncturist I worked predominantly in a job where I felt my chest closing to protect my heart, and in relation to this my arms were becoming locked by my sides (the arms are energetically an extension of your heart). Dancing regularly and putting my attention back in my body, I became aware of this and it afforded my body the time and space to release some of this tension and return back to balance. However, even dancing once or twice a week and doing yoga and other heart opening practices, I was struggling to counteract the strains of my work.

Fortunately, nowadays my occupational choices are actually a reflection of my heart so I don't have the same problem, but I've no doubt that many people around me get similarly locked through chronic exposure to discordant situations and experiences.

And then there is just the general stress of modern living. After doing a lot of typing or carrying heavy shopping bags around town we may wring out or shake out our hands, which may be wracked with tension, but what about the tension we feel in our whole body after a day in urban life on Planet Earth? Even without a specific stress source, just being in a city with all the electromagnetic stresses and absence of nature and natural frequencies stresses the body.

It's also worth noting that in the natural world after a stressful experience animals shake to disperse tension. We might often make a joke about someone going on a dance floor and 'shaking their stuff', but absolutely sometimes it's exactly what we need to do to clear our energy field and dissolve stress.

So letting the whole body move, regularly, can help to alleviate acute and chronic patterns of stress which can affect the body and posture through repeated engagement, such as through our job or relationships.

Effect on the mind

As mentioned in Chapter 5, free dancing is also a wonderful practice for keeping your perception fine-tuned to your broader sense of self, including your spontaneous instincts and emotions and not becoming overly aligned with the smaller more rigid mind as being 'who you are'. We also touched earlier on how Gabrielle Roth identified dancing as a great practice for bringing your thoughts, feelings and actions back into congruent alignment, so we can see benefits of dance occur on many levels!

This is because free dancing helps to balance the left and right brain – with the left brain being more aligned to the intellect, and the right brain to the senses and broader perception of self.

This is important as the terms of reference for the smaller, ego mind is created through past experiences as it cannot perceive that which is new and it hasn't yet experienced, so if you become too aligned with it, you can become a bit rigid in your thinking and miss what's actually going on in front of you – where life is happening!

So when we engage with our broader self, and include in our awareness our relationship and interactions with the world around, it can give us a greater sense of flow to our path and direction in life, and enrich it greatly with a sense of adventure and growth.

Conversely if you stay too aligned to what's happened in the past you can withdraw from the flow of what is actually happening now and jump back to how you *think* things should be! Follow the mind and things can tend to stay the same; follow the broader self and things can tend to change!

This state of perception and alignment from which we often perceive could also be referred to as our 'assemblage point'. So, changing our perception from that of the smaller ego dialogue mind to one which relates more to our spontaneous instinctive capacities could be said to be a shift of assemblage point, our vantage point on life.

I often experience this broader perspective while I'm actually dancing as my mental landscape changes, but there are also occasions where I feel that I really connect to expressing in words the experience of where dancing can take me! Once, while attending a 5Rhythms workshop, after a couple of days, the workshop leader asked us to sit down, and starting with the words 'When I dance' just to then carry on writing. I seem to remember just writing those three words as being more or less the only thing which came out from any part of my normal mind and then my hand just went in a blur across the page with my logical mind somewhere in my back pocket and the rest of what came out I think sort of even surprised me...

When I dance my body feels, lighter, more energised fluid state of healing dissipation of negativity enjoyment self-awareness holy sacred being of light be released to form expression to show the way and the meaning of each moment of light in life each moment of being is according to the energetic rhythms and the ability to dance with them move with them set them free inside your soul, to move is to be as one to be fluid is to be love you know exactly what to do open and let the light and love shine the spirit dance manifest in body, manifest in life each moment.
When I dance my heart feels opened loved like poetry and magic in action a freedom which it craves in each moment, each moment demands the clarity of expression afforded through dance, the clarity of love and all within it be manifest through dance and allowing to be in tune with ONE's heart and express it so.
Richard Brook, 2005

So if you spend enough time doing practices like free dance which align you to this bigger version of yourself, then you start to understand that the smaller mind is something that just sits inside of you. You move your seat of consciousness from being in the terrified realms of the ego mind – and occasionally venturing into the broader self – and into being the broader self where now the vagaries of the ego mind might occasionally kick in!

See you on a dance floor!

Authentic movement

Authentic Movement was originated by Mary Starks Whitehouse in the 1950s. I find it can be a particularly effective practice for promoting heart energy as it facilitates non-judgemental movement and observation – which is the essence of how the heart perceives!

The mover participates with their eyes closed, and without music to guide them. This enables them to really tune in with their inner experience, and be moved by the rhythms of it, rather than the rhythms of music from outside which often accompany movement practices.

The practice also occurs in a circle of witnesses, who are encouraged to observe from this non-judgemental, heart open perspective. This helps 'contain' and envelop those movers within the circle with the compassionate heart energy which resonates from the witness's body – as we discussed in Chapter 2, the heart has an expansive electromagnetic field. This helps facilitate and catalyse, through resonance, the movers to move from a similar heart space. As a mover therefore you have the ideal conditions to move spontaneously and authentically.

Each mover is paired with a witness and then there is a mutual feedback session at the end where each person relays their experience of either moving or witnessing. This is done without judgement or interpretation, as the focus is solely on the direct mental, emotional and physical experience without the mind creating narrative on it.

As the feedback is done without judgement there is an added sense of security without being fearful of potential criticism.

Sound therapy, music, singing and Taoist healing sounds

We've discussed in depth the influence on the body and nervous system of vibration, so music, sound therapy and indeed singing can all be strongly therapeutic activities. As we mentioned everyone has a unique vibration profile which gives you unique preferences – just think of how certain types of music can have some people jumping around, while others wish they could turn it off!

So trust your impulses about what music you are drawn to; it can often be because that vibration is soothing for you and your soul, as an individual.

Sound therapy works in a slightly more structured way, again using recognised frequencies and vibrations which help to heal the body, but which may not have quite the same 'personal and cultural resonance' for you that music has.

And singing can also be particularly therapeutic. It's often in our instinct to make the sounds, which we need to harmonise and balance our subtle energies, so trust what wishes to come out of your mouth!

Unfortunately, we can get shut down in our vocal expression, as we are often judged about whether we can 'sing' or not at an early age and this can stick to our self-perception. But everyone can make spontaneous healing sounds and should be encouraged to do so – whether you can sing in tune isn't important in this context, so it's unfortunate that being 'branded' when you are younger tends to sit heavy in the mind.

Sometimes you also just have to 'fake it till you make it' in the sense that when you start to alleviate some of that tension around being vocal, getting used to singing, it can then spontaneously flow more easily.

If singing really feels off your radar (even in the shower) it's a well-known Taoist healing practice to make particular sounds that correspond to the functions of organs in order to balance them. I'll list them below, but it's worthy of further research (look up Taoist Healing Sounds) to learn the subtleties of the practice, as the sounds often correspond to movements. It's generally recommended to repeat each sound up to six times initially.

Liver	Shuu
Heart	Haaa
Spleen	Whoo
Lung	Tsss
Kidney	Fuu

Common issues of imbalance

Distraction and avoidance (of feeling)

When there is a sensation or feeling within us, some communication from within that we don't want to experience, it can lead itself to choosing to distract your attention onto other things to avoid feeling it. The problem with this is it obviously lends itself to other potential health problems, as some of the methods of distraction, which vary from drink and drugs to food and TV addictions, aren't usually very healthy! And the feeling and sensation is often still sitting there in the subconscious. So having regular times when you spend quality time with yourself or explain to others how you are is very beneficial as it can stop these feelings from creeping in without being acknowledged and either treated or actioned. The conscious path is a brave path, but ultimately a rewarding one.

Fatigue and lack of energy

When we don't listen to ourselves and respect our basic needs then it can create fatigue.

On one level it can look as if fatigue originates from two sources. Firstly, when we don't give ourselves the circumstances around us that nourish us we become energetically deficient. A great deal of our nourishment in life comes from more than just food – it comes from what we engage with – and as we spoke about in Chapter 2, when you are doing what you love you feel much more energised due to the infusion of soul energy into your body. So even if you are trying to prop yourself up with the most amazing super foods it wouldn't help, as it's the absence of soul food that is missing! Similarly if you were trying to rest it wouldn't help either, as the problem is the deficiency of input, a kind of 'spirit level' malnutrition.

Secondly, with fatigue it can also be an internal imbalance (what we call an internal 'block') which is creating the problem. When your energy gets shut down and drained like this it can be quite frightening (I've experienced this personally) as it sometimes doesn't seem to matter what you do, how much rest you get, or what you eat, you can't seem to generate any energy. With this type of situation it's worth looking at how much stress and tension you are under, since tension uses up a massive amount of energy.

Tension consumes energy

Try clenching your fist tightly for a few seconds – it soon gets tired! Now think about how much tension we often carry in our body when we are stressed. And tension doesn't just inhabit external fascia and muscles; it also inhabits internal organs.

So, think how much energy we often waste, and by association reduce the amount available to us to do what we love, because it's wrapped up in tension throughout the body. Any tension held in the body takes energy.

Let's take another example. Think about something that makes you angry, or maybe adopt the body pose and body characteristics of when you feel angry. You will notice it involves a degree of muscle contraction and tension, clenching of arms, sometimes fists, jutting jaw, a generalised tension. This can be necessary, indeed instinctual, as an appropriate response, but consider the amount of energy it consumes if you are chronically angry, or chronically exposed to a situation that prompts anger. There may be an event that has occurred where the expression has stayed unprocessed within. So we have to be very careful with unexpressed emotions as they can get stuck within the body and drain us.

Another dynamic which can be involved in the creation of fatigue is where we also seek to try and block the signals from the various organs and elements in the body which are trying to talk to us by locking the body up so we don't hear those signals. This again is where tension can be created.

The manifestation of this response is very similar to where the body is tensing up to protect itself from external circumstances that are discordant and harmful. In this case you can end up in a situation where there is a great deal of energy being directed to feed the tension to avoid feeling your own feelings inside, rather than being directed into creating a healthier lifestyle!

The bottom line with any of the issues outlined above, though, is that when you prime your awareness, start to listen to the deeper levels of your intelligence and understand the signals coming from your body, you will feel more empowered to make the choices which support your wellbeing. No matter whether it's an internal or external problem, you will become sharp enough to realise it's happening and hear the call of your instincts to create balance again.

It wasn't until I started regularly practising yoga, and experiencing the relaxation at the end of class, that I began to realise that my default state had become one of tension – I'd just gotten used to it. By regularly having that blissful 20 minutes of deep relaxation at the end of class, that state of relaxation then started to feel much more like the norm, and I could also see what activities, jobs and relationships would then make me tighten back up again.

All the therapies we have discussed in this section can be helpful at alleviating tension. But modalities such as yoga and meditation can enable you to alleviate tension, and because of the strong introspective aspect, can also enable you to see what areas of your life might be contributing to them so you can do something about it!

Diet, eating and digestion

Diet is such a huge arena, and with so many conflicting viewpoints it often appears possible that you can make a case for eating virtually anything! If you think of the scope of dietary choices out there – all the way from the Inuit who survive predominantly on meat and fish through to veganism – then it can be tricky to draw generalisations.

Given that there are so many different possibilities of dietary style out there, we need to simplify things down – and get back into the body – because that is what is unique to you. No one has the same physiology as you. No one had the same upbringing as you. No one sat with you and your family when you were growing up and developing and so no one knows exactly what foods nourish you in what way.

I'll be clear with this. I've treated many people (and had my own problems) with dietary imbalances, particularly as a result of what I would call eating 'prescribed diets' where someone is following what they *think* they should eat rather than following their body's own innate intelligence.

This can be equally as pathological as many other conditions, as you could be making yourself unwell through eating from an idea of what you think you need, rather than what you actually need.

Diet can be such a difficult area. The physiological, emotional and mental stress we can subject ourselves to with diet is huge. As a society we struggle very badly with diet, as it overspills and interconnects with so many other areas of our life, so it gets affected by our social life, our emotions, our beliefs. This is the whole essence of holistic wellness – parts of our life interconnect and one aspect affects another – so looking at diet as the root of a problem is also often missing the point.

One of the most hazardous situations I observe with people when it comes to diet is when they first start to explore, they may read something and start to follow a suggested diet, and then get 'hooked' on that approach, and fail to transition again when the body starts to give off signals of imbalance.

For example, if someone is used to eating quite a heavy and rich diet, such as a more traditional British diet, and they pick up a book suggesting a raw food diet, then chances are that initially they may well feel better, as the body appreciates a lighter load once in a while and has a chance to cleanse and benefit from the live enzyme content of the food.

However, a little while down the track this diet may be vastly imbalanced for that person and the body calls for the reintegration of richer foods again, but if the person is 'hooked' on the 'idea' of what they think they should be eating then they have a problem, which generally becomes a neurosis, confusion, and a lack of comfort and pleasure in the body.

So once you have pushed the door open to exploring different dietary perspectives, in some ways you are better knowing more than less, since greater knowledge can give a greater sense of permission to choose what is actually right for you.

I'll repeat again – as I see it so often – try to avoid getting hooked on one dietary structure or philosophy in your mind as being the ultimate 'objective' truth as this limits the scope of you understanding and responding to your body's signals. It could be the subjective truth for you, which is great if you have figured that out, but becoming rigid could come back and bite you (pardon the pun) at some point.

So the position I always come back to with diet is that each person is unique and you have to find what works for you. However, to do this, it can also be worth experimenting a little so you can consciously work out what works for you.

You always have to consider with diet that, just like everything else I teach, there are two aspects: (1) what you are putting into your body from the 'outside' – the nutritional aspect of what you eat, and (2) how well you are on the 'inside' – the functioning of the digestive system.

What tends to happen is we overly focus on the nutritional aspect of food without giving enough attention to how well our digestion is working. You can be eating all the best foods in the world, but if you are totally stressed out in your life and your digestion isn't working properly, or you are eating food that doesn't suit you, then it will inhibit the benefit. And it's then very easy to 'blame' the food, without addressing your inner digestive efficiency.

As stated before, it's very difficult to give definitive nutritional advice, since every person is different, but there are some helpful digestive points which can apply in a broader sense to most people.

So I'm now going to present a few different dietary pointers which I have found over time to be fairly solid principles regarding healthy eating that you could try out and see if they make sense for you. Some are principles which are applicable across a broad range of people, such as eating breakfast, whereas others are more specific which you could take or leave depending on their relevance to you. You may find that trying a few things out could help you fine-tune what's right for you. I acknowledge that some of the points contradict each other; that's the whole point of what I've been discussing with diet: there is very little that's black or white!

Considerations when planning what you eat

1. **Type of food** – Is it what your body really wants, instinctively? Or just an 'idea' you have from your intellect?
2. **Quality of food** – Is the food fresh, full of life force, organic? Or packaged, full of additives?
3. **How are you?** In the present situation, are you relaxed, able to chew, give attention to, and digest your food? Are you in good company so you feel nourished by the entire experience? Or running around full of tension and adrenalin, sitting at your desk, distracted, etc?
4. **Ease of digestion** – All the above points could be positive, but you need to consider the ease of digestion and food combining of what you have eaten. For example, eating a starchy starter followed by a large amount of animal protein (particularly fish) and then throwing rapidly on top ice cream, cheese and biscuits, etc., can be very taxing on the digestion! Particularly if point 3 above is also compromised!
5. **Preparation** – Consider the subtle impact of the person preparing the food. Are they infusing it with love or stress? (Remember how a person's energy field extends from their body, and in this case over your food!)

Digestive considerations

Be relaxed
When your adrenals are switched on your digestive secretions decrease (your body is in fight or flight).

Chew properly
You digest proteins in your stomach but carbs in your mouth via the enzyme secretions there (so chew your food properly).

If you really struggle with digesting foods – particularly in stress – you may wish to utilise food combining principles (see 'Dietary "structures"' later on).

Don't drink water with meals

Also avoid drinking water alongside your meal as it dilutes the digestive enzymes mentioned above. Green tea and fennel tea after a meal can be beneficial in the right quantity as they stimulate your conjugation enzymes that help digestion. Too much green tea is to be cautioned against, though, as it's a diuretic. Using loose green tea is beneficial as you can moderate the quantity.

Eat at regular intervals

Eat at regular intervals, preferably at the same time each day – your body develops a circadian rhythm of secreting enzymes and gearing up to eat in a regular pattern. When it goes awry it affects not just eating but digestion, sleep, and your overall sense of wellbeing.

Eat breakfast

Missing breakfast sets off a chain reaction in the body of stimulating the adrenals so our resources come from that 'empty' energy which also depletes our digestion secretions further so we then become reliant on stimulant foods for 'quick win' energy which are often full of sugar and create blood sugar spikes and a vicious cycle begins.

Eat fruit separately

Eat fruit separately from other foods, or else it ferments in your digestive tract and can proliferate bad bacteria. It can also force other foods through the intestines before they are properly digested as it has a much quicker transit time.

Eat in season

Eat in season for the fruits and veg that are indigenous to your climate; nature knows best and creation manifests to balance. Sweet fruits are indigenous to hotter countries – beware eating too much of them in colder damp countries.

Beware too much raw

Beware too much raw food, particularly in colder seasons. It stresses the spleen which essentially has to then reheat the food and break it down. In effect, cooked food has already become partially digested.

Live enzyme quality

Stay conscious of the live enzyme composition within food. Packaged food tends to be dead – no live enzymes (prana/qi) whereas fresh produce still has life force! And the live enzymes can help the digestive process and break down cooked foods. Eating some raw food before meals is thought to neutralise the 'pathological leucocytosis' response which is the rise in white blood cells prompted by food heated at very high temperatures or food that was processed and refined. (Essentially where your body feels it is being invaded.)

Be appetised!

Consistently eating food that doesn't really stimulate your appetite also isn't healthy as it suppresses enzyme secretions to break the food down. Think of how some food 'whets your appetite' – that's a stimulation of your digestive enzymes.

When we aren't really keen on a food this doesn't tend to happen so effectively. My own analogy is that food is a bit like music: just because a type of music is 'technically better' doesn't mean that it's to your taste – if you were consistently forced to listen to it, it wouldn't be good for you!

Some sweetness is healthy

Cutting out sugar does not mean cutting out all sweetness from your diet! Do not confuse refined sugar with sweetness. The body needs the resonance of sweetness – it supports the stomach and spleen (see 'Five Elements Diet' below) – but refined sugar overloads it.

Beware obsession

Beware of becoming obsessed with diet. This kind of neurosis is often indicative of a greater imbalance in our life where we are generally undernourished on other levels of our being. Comfort eating is often the result of a lack of nurture and heart nourishment. We can derive energy through supportive interaction in our life, and natural environments. The absence of this tends to mean we overemphasise food consumption.

The context of food nutrition

To elaborate further on the final point above, a core teaching of this work is that we require a range of inputs in our life to feel abundant and full of energy. We need to be doing what we love, instinctively avoiding things that drain us, and getting enough rest and support. All these things affect our energy levels, but when they fall out of balance we can tend to blame and overemphasise food.

Reflect on the section on relationships and the chemistry and alchemy of what happens when we have contact with other people; it has the capacity to really energise. Often when this nourishing contact is missing, at the heart level, we try and hit the food instead to make up for the deficiency, the same as when we are in a job we don't like; we can be picking at food to try and lift our energy levels up. (The converse can of course also be true: we can overemphasise getting energy from work and relationships, and excessive rest if we don't nurture ourselves with food properly too.) Always try and keep the holistic picture! Optimise every level of your life.

Dietary 'structures'

As I've emphasised several times, there are a lot of apparent contradictions in dietary advice, but if you did wish to try and align with a particular dietary pattern you might want to give the following ideas some consideration. These structures may also help you understand or give validity to what your natural tendency might be. For example, if you really want to be a vegetarian, but find yourself desiring meat, it could well be that this makes sense in light of the blood type diet – that you have a blood type which suits eating meat.

As ever, though, I would caution with any of the below not to be too strict; your needs change and your body knows best.

Mealtime quantities
Eat breakfast like a King, Lunch like a Prince and Dinner like a Pauper is an often used adage from American

nutritionist Adelle Davis in the 1950s[24]. This philosophy sits in alignment with our digestive capacity, which is greater earlier in the day than later. However, we can tend to ignore this as we often have sedentary day jobs which don't stimulate the metabolism to kick in and burn the fuel in the morning and then we comfort eat a big meal later in the day instead. Also contributing to this tendency for a larger evening meal is that it can also provide an opportunity for social connection, helping to make up for what can be a lack of quality connection during the day, compounded by a general sense of malnourishment from our day in general, particularly if our work might be draining too. Following from the above, a big meal later in the day then means we feel less like breakfast in the morning again, which perpetuates a vicious cycle of eating more later in the evening, and the circadian rhythm can then contribute to keeping us a bit stuck in that pattern. So in order to break this pattern and adopt Adelle Davis's recommendation, there can be a few challenges, but it can be a beneficial philosophy.

Eating according to blood type

The Blood Type Diet[25] recommends eating in accordance with your blood type. For example, if you have blood type A it means you come from the Agrarian Revolution genetic pool, which means you have a more alkaline constitution, which means you are more suited to a high carb and grains diet. Blood type O means you come from the Hunter Gatherer genetic pool, which means you have a more acidic constitution and are more suited to a diet with animal protein. Blood type B is recommended to have a diverse diet, but should still avoid particular grains and meats, and blood type

AB can eat the foods that types A and B can eat but should be careful around food combining them as they typically have low stomach acid.

Food combining diet

As we discussed above, you digest proteins in the stomach with acidic enzymes and starchy carbs in the mouth with alkaline enzymes so some people advocate eating proteins and starchy carbs separately. Using food combining principles to various degrees can also be helpful if you are under stress and you feel your digestive efficiency is compromised. Then when the stress alleviates you can return back to your more natural patterns.

The Body Ecology Diet

The Body Ecology Diet[26] pays great attention to digestive efficiency. Promotes the removal in particular of refined sugars from the diet which proliferate bad bacteria (like candida) and using fermented foods and products to support good bacteria. Similar to food combining diets, using the Body Ecology Diet principles can be useful if your digestive efficiency is being compromised through stress.

The Five Elements Diet

The Five Elements Diet (from Chinese medicine): The Five Elements Diet works on the principle that each organ (or pair of organs in the body that comprise a particular element) is supported by the resonance of a particular taste. For example the liver and gall bladder are supported by the taste of sour. Kidney and bladder = salty. Heart and small intestine = bitter. Stomach and spleen = sweetness. Lungs and large intestine = pungent. This explains why we often instinctively desire particular tastes, as it's our body giving us information about what it needs to balance. This also explains why we often continue eating long after we actually feel full – it's because we haven't got the hit of a particular flavour we need to balance ourselves. For example, we often eat a huge meal and follow it with a sweet desert. This clearly isn't because we need more calories, it's because the stomach and spleen are actually struggling to process what you have eaten, so desire something that tastes sweet as this actually helps support the function of the organ.

Therefore understanding the principles of the Five Elements Diet, you may also get an indication of your internal state depending on what flavours you reach out for. For example, if you start desiring (or avoiding) lots of salty food, it can be an indication of an imbalance in the kidney and bladder, and again your body trying to instinctively balance.

The Five Elements Diet can also be seen to go some way to understanding apparent contradictions in dietary advice that may exist elsewhere. For example, some dietary recommendations may say to avoid dairy foods but the lungs and large intestine are actually supported by the resonance of pungent tastes, such as from cheese. So the diet can explain why we are not only drawn to certain foods, but indeed, why they may actually be beneficial to us to help keep our balance.

Fasting

If you want to really stretch your perception regarding diet, then you may want to try a fast of some kind. Not only can these be beneficial for our physical health, but on other levels too.

Commonly our default pattern, for example, is to eat three meals per day, every day without fail and without a period of conscious abstention. We often don't appreciate exactly the role that food is playing in not just our physical health, but also our emotional and mental health.

Having facilitated programmes at a juice fasting retreat, Moinhos Velhos, for a number of years (where you just drink juice for between 7 and 14 days in order to cleanse and detoxify) it's not uncommon for people in attendance to feed back how the programme makes them more conscious of their reliance on food and how much time they spend focusing on it. I'll hasten to add, that feedback doesn't usually come because they are feeling hungry whilst doing the programme, actually far from it.

Because the juice fasting programmes, although absent of solid food, are so nourishing in terms of their activities and group spirit, they highlight for people how they often rely on food in their everyday life to make up for a deficiency of energy and vibrancy from their general life situation. For example, if you are in the habit of picking up two chocolate bars on your way home from a stressful day at work, this can often become ingrained in your psyche as a norm, and as a need. You might even get agitated if the shop runs out of your favourite brand.

A few days away from that environment, in a natural space full of light, high vibration energy and nourishing activity, you start to see the pattern for what it is – it's not a default, it's not your objective norm, it's simply a pattern you have developed relative to that *stressful* context of your regular life.

We see this a lot at the retreat, not just with food, but with other addictions and habits too. People sometimes attend the programmes who've been heavily reliant on drink or cigarettes in their regular lives, and then are surprised when that pattern seemingly disappears when they attend the programmes, which can help the participant see that it's not an absolute need, just a relative need. And of course this can then generate the confidence, and a new template, for how they wish their regular life to be on the other side of the retreat.

My first experience of intentional abstention around food taught me a massive amount. I was attending a Drum dance (similar to Sun Moon Dances which were also envisioned by Native American mystic Joseph Rael) where you dance intermittently for two days without food and water. To most people the idea of this would likely fall somewhere between challenging and absurd and even to me the idea was somewhat confronting as at the time I'd never experienced anything similar either (I later went on to regularly dance at Sun Moon Dances which are a day longer). And while they aren't always plain sailing, they certainly make you conscious that a lot of the limitations we place on ourselves in terms of what we think we are capable of are simply self-imposed and based on a collective 'norm'. By even challenging and stretching your self-imposed beliefs and limitations around food consumption you could be making a start in understanding that you are something much bigger than a lot of the belief systems that inhabit your mind.

If you are intending to explore fasting, I would heartily recommend initially doing so very lightly, such as with intermittent fasting, or ideally in a supervised programme such as at a juice detox retreat. And of course, if you have any medical concerns you should seek the advice of your medical professional first. As we discussed earlier, when you are stressed your digestive efficiency is compromised, so giving the digestion a break to catch up periodically can be helpful.

However, in this situation you have to recognise that the fasting isn't the answer to the stress. While it's helping your digestion to balance, you should always still be looking to identify and optimise any areas of your life that are creating the undue stress in the first place.

I would also recommend that you make a one-off attempt at fasting to begin with, so that you can return to following your body instinct around food in a free-flowing fashion afterwards, while integrating the experiences of fasting into your body-mind.

I mention this as a short period of intentional abstention can also quickly turn into an excess rigidity around diet and become something that can feed an obsessive element of the psyche around control, which clearly isn't good either! Whilst we don't want to become a glutton in our eating patterns, we also don't want to become excessively rigid either. What we are looking for is perspective and self-awareness around our habits, and a period of eating lightly or abstaining can help to build this, alongside the physical benefits of giving the digestion a break.

As my acupuncture teacher once said, "moderation in all things, including moderation!"

Suggestions

I'm not big on making actual nutritional recommendations, for all the reasons outlined above, but there are a few suggestions I've found over time to be hugely useful.

- Porridge for breakfast rather than a sugary cereal. If you find it dull then throw some muesli or granola on top to make it more interesting.

- Udo's Oil (a mixture of omega fats in the correct ratio for your body needs): Essential fatty acids support healthy cell function alongside glands, organs and tissues. As a result this also benefits healthy cardiovascular, brain and nerve function. Since this product is full of good fats (HDLs) they also emulsify and help lower cholesterol. EFAs also absorb the vibration of sunlight which makes them tremendously helpful for those who suffer with winter blues – as if you've taken it during the sunnier seasons its energy will stay with you. I actually recommend putting Udo's Oil into your breakfast porridge too! N.B. If you can't purchase Udo's Oil then search for a similar omega 3, 6, 9 blend.

- Goji berries: They have been used in Chinese medicine for over 2,000 years. There are reports that goji berries were steeped in hot water and eaten by monks in the Himalayan mountains thousands of years ago to help aid meditation and obtain greater health, vitality, longevity, energy and stamina. Also put a few of these in your breakfast and you will be good to go for the rest of the day!

General healthy living and working tips

So many working environments in the modern world can place undue stress on the system, so here are a few healthy pointers!

The benefits of nature and negative ions

Within any natural living matter there is a tiny micro-vibration, which by its nature is recognised and harmonious to the body since it's in all living matter – including us!

Modern urban areas not only have a deficiency of this natural vibration, but of course are also predominated by man-made electromagnetic energies and vibrations that can be subtly abrasive to our subtle energies and create stress.

KEY POINT

Getting out into 'nature' is good for you. It is essentially your natural habitat, although becoming accustomed to urban dwelling we tend to think of nature as being somewhat 'alternative'.

Alongside the harmonious micro-vibration to our own body that natural settings provide, another aspect of the healthy environment that a natural setting, or natural life provides, is that of negative ions. The air around us contains ion particles, and any natural environment has an abundance of negative ion particles (despite their name, 'negative' ions are seen as the healthy ones, and 'positive' ions the unhealthy ones).

Negative ions predominate in natural environments, such as forests, the countryside, streams, and mountains. They are particularly high in places where there is running and rushing water, which, alongside explaining why we often feel so much more refreshed after being out in nature, also explains why we often feel so much more refreshed after a shower, swim, or after it has rained.

The extra proliferation of negative ions around water is the effect of water evaporation, and the breaking of surface tension of water. For example, the normal ion count in fresh country air is around 2,000 to 4,000 negative ions per cubic centimetre. At places with rushing water, for example Yosemite Falls in the U.S., the ion count can increase to over 100,000 negative ions per cubic centimetre.[27]

This compares to polluted environments, such as a motorway during rush hour, where the level can fall to as "low as 100 negative ions per cubic centimetre"[28]. Other producers of positive ions are indoors where TV or computer monitors are operating, where air has flowed through ductwork such as in air-conditioning units[29] and environments of warm, dry winds[30].

Indeed, the World Health Organization also acknowledges that indoor spaces can often be debilitating to our health, with Jan Stolwijk stating that "there is probably more damage done to human health by indoor air pollution than by outdoor pollution". Most of us are inside for 70% to 80% of our time.[31]

So given all these factors, and particularly how much time we often spend indoors, heading outdoors, to negative ion rich environments, as often as possible is extremely beneficial.

For more on negative ions please visit this blog: Nature and Negative Ions[xxi]

The challenges of modern work environments

So we can see that modern urban environments with polluted air and a preponderance of technological devices are a mass

xxi   www.creativewellness.co.uk/bookblogs

producer of the unhealthy positive ions. Urban based offices in particular can also be very challenging.

How this relates to us is that we, due to interaction with our environment, get affected by these positive ions. We absorb energy from our environment, and in the case of polluted positive ions they will affect us, being absorbed into our organs. The air we breathe is absorbed into our lungs and our blood and is circulated around our whole body, affecting every system. Polluted energies cause the body to work harder and use more energy to maintain balance.

KEY POINT

In order to clear the effects of positive ions and discordant electromagnetic energy, try to leave the office at breaks, shower when you return home and often head out into the countryside. Another tip is to have plants in your office.

The importance of sunlight

Our brain chemistry requires certain spectral rays of sunlight to hit our retina (it also goes some way to our brain recognising it's actually daytime!) and these rays do not pass through glass. So in an office environment there might be lots of windows, but it's likely you're not quite getting what you need.

KEY POINT

Step outside or open a window if possible and let natural light hit your eyes, absolutely essential in the winter too with even shorter days.

Sleep

As explained earlier, going 'inwards' and resting is fundamental in our life 'yin' and 'yang' cycle.

So here are some helpful tips for getting a better night's sleep.

Try to avoid being on your laptop/phone/watching TV late at night. All these devices give off electromagnetic energy which disturbs the body and irritates the hypothalamus of the brain. Hence they 'trance us out'. Notice how after about 15 minutes on a laptop you are 'hooked in' – you lose awareness of sensation in your body, whether you are hungry/thirsty/tired, etc.

In addition, try not to eat within two or three hours of bedtime. If your body is doing lots of processing of food it can't be getting on with the other essential tasks it needs to do overnight.

If there is a lot of light pollution where you live, try to sleep in a pitch-black room – it will help with your brain chemistry.

Finally, alcohol stresses out your liver, which is massively active during the night processing and cleaning your blood. If you drink alcohol regularly at night you will place extra stress on your liver which often impairs the quality of sleep. You may still fall asleep exhausted, but the quality is affected.

Movement

Following our earlier tutorials around yin and yang, certain organs within the body require you to move around for them to function most effectively.

KEY POINT

Make sure you lead an active and healthy life!

8

And Finally!

And finally, let's sum up!

We've discussed what we are actually trying to achieve here on Planet Earth and the rules of the game.

And while acknowledging there are a huge number of other perspectives on life – and feel free to form your own – here's what we've boiled it down to.

You are here to radiate the gifts of your soul out into the world around you. This radiance, which comes through the heart, acts in tandem with the forces of nature such as yin and yang and the Five Elements to give your soul purpose balanced form. As you start to live by the will of your heart and soul, you become a soulful radiant being, with your soul radiance imprinted onto your fluids, your flesh and your bones, the wisdom of your soul infused into every pore, driving out old stagnant patterns and habits, easing them out of your life. You act in flow with nature's laws to stay balanced.

Your soul imprint becomes so strong that the genetic tendencies you were born with and old patterns from early (and earlier) life begin to be transcended, dispersed, and your personality no longer acts as an empty carriage for these old stories. Instead your personality is the joyous vehicle that carries the nuances of your soul and you marvel at the unique gift you were given from your ancestors to enable you to carry out your life's work doing what you love.

You skilfully use the natural and healing arts and activities, which come in many forms, to consciously access the universal intelligence of creation which passes through all living beings. As a human being you are lucky that you have both natural instinct, and the ability to consciously attune to it, so you use that faculty wisely when you feel you are coming off balance.

This is who you truly are. You are on that journey, and remember, it's not a destination! Listen closely to what I've written; it's about finding ways to get closer to your true self, which happens moment to moment, and if you are doing that then you are on the right path and that's all you can ever do!

So, all I'd ask, if you've found this information useful, is you spread the word or pass this book around! You are welcome to join my community at www.creativewellness.co.uk and find out how we can work together with treatments, talks, classes and retreats. I love sharing this wisdom!

We may not all need a manual for our washing machines, since, let's face it, we don't all have one, but who out there doesn't need a manual for life?

You are and forever will be the only you. Live it well, my friend.

About Richard

Richard is founder of Creative Wellness, and a specialist in Five Element acupuncture, Dru yoga, meditation, holistic education and the body-mind connection. He's passionate about understanding and creating what you need to have a successful life, measured from the deepest level of your own perception, not through achieving in the eyes of others.

With over 20 years of experience, he is a true holistic expert. He graduated the renowned College of Traditional Acupuncture and went on to have successful practices in the Midlands, Bristol and latterly London.

Alongside this he developed his Creative Yoga brand into one of London's most unique and exciting yoga projects, organising and teaching some of the capital's biggest and most unique events. Understanding people's holistic needs as ever, there was also a strong emphasis on connection and community, with events like singles and couples yoga and Yoga Rave London which also had in-built social elements, rare in the yoga world where people often exit with barely a glance at those they have been in class with.

He has a successful corporate arm to his business, designing and delivering wellness programmes and managing a team of teachers who attend businesses throughout London.

He also works internationally, helping facilitate programmes at the world renowned Moinhos Velhos Juice Detox Retreat, contributing to it becoming rated amongst the top 10 detox retreats in the world by *The Times*!

His wellness blog is one of the best of its kind, demonstrating his broad-reaching knowledge, experience and passion to share what can be of help to others.

He has helped thousands of clients, been featured across many media channels, and organised and taught at many high-profile events.

Endnotes

1   Soul embodied/embodied presence refers to where you feel fully present within the body. It is often used specifically in reference to essentially grounding the faculties of the soul throughout the personality, character, tendencies and instincts.

2   'One' (with a capital O) refers to a vast sense of connection with everything around you on every level.

3   When you are energetically connected you have a connection beyond the realms of physical boundaries and constraints.

4   The word etheric "is a derivative from the word ether, which has been considered a medium that permeates space, transmitting transverse waves of energy" (https://www.consciouslifestylemag.com/human-energy-field-aura/).

5   Energetic body describes the various layers of subtle vibrating energy that surrounds living beings, beyond the more evident physical layer. (These layers include the etheric body, emotional body, lower and higher mental bodies, causal body, soul body and integrated spiritual body; see https://www.crystalherbs.com/chakras-subtle-bodies.asp). The energy body can hold information – subtle vibrations – of various degrees of density that are picked up from the surrounding matter. Vibrations in the energy field can be felt and interpreted via the mind as thoughts and feelings, and there is also a degree of interaction between the energy body and the physical body via the chakra system, which acts as a mechanism for how vibrations in the energy field can enter the body.

6   *Hidden Messages in Water*, Masaru Emoto. Pocket Books; New edition, 2005

7   For Mark Walsh's video, 'Trolls of learning', go to https://www.youtube.com/watch?v=lKGR_hxyomo

8   *Being and Vibration: Entering the new world*, Joseph Rael. Millichap Books, 2015

9   For more on chakra associations, see https://www.essential-reiki.com/chakra-symbols-color.html and http://satoriconnections.com/M18/Chakras/SoundChakraMantras.htm

10 For more on quantum theory, see https://www.learning-mind.com/quantum-mechanics-reveals-how-we-are-all-truly-connected/, https://www.starstuffs.com/physcon/intro.html, https://www.collective-evolution.com/2013/01/20/quantum-entanglement-what-it-is-and-why-its-relevant/

11   https://en.wikipedia.org/wiki/Yin_and_yang

12   *In Perfect Timing: Memoirs of a Man for the New Millennium*, Peter Caddy. Findhorn Press, 1996

13   *Movement Medicine: How to Awaken, Dance and Live your Dreams*, Ya'Acov Darling Khan, Susannah Darling Khan. Hay House UK, 2009. Thanks to Ya'Acov Darling Khan for his permission to include his words in this book. For further information on Ya'Acov Darling Khan, see his website www.darlingkhan.com

14   *Karma and Sexuality: The Transforming Energies of Spiritual Development*, Zulma Reyo. Ashgrove, 2001; *Philosophia Perennis, Vol 1. Speaking on the Golden Verses of Pythagoras*. Edition 1, Bhagwan Shree Rajneesh. Rajneesh Foundation, 1981

15   *Maps to Ecstasy: A Healing Journey for the Untamed Spirit* (illustrated and revised edition), Gabrielle Roth, John Loudon. New World Library, 1998, pp. 19 & 195

16   Angeles Arrien, *The Four-Fold Way: Walking the Paths of the Warrior, Teacher, Healer, and Visionary*, quoted in Gabrielle Roth, *Maps to Ecstasy: The Healing Power of Movement*. New World Library, 1998, pp. xv–xvi (bold added for emphasis)

17   *Super-Learning*, Sheila Ostrander and Lynn Schroeder. Laurel, 1982

18   Julie Visaka Hotchkiss, *Dru Yoga Teacher Training Book 5*. Thanks to Julie Visaka Hotchkiss and Dru Yoga for their agreement to include her quote in this book.

19   *Timeless Healing: The Power and Biology of Belief*, Herbert Benson M.D. Scribner; First Fireside edition, 1997, p. 133

20   Dr. Herbert Benson, The Institute for Mind Body Medicine, http://www.relaxationresponse.org/fightorflight.htm

21   Sri Sri Ravi Shankar, https://www.artofliving.org/meditation/meditation-for-you/meditation-sleep

22   *The Book of Secrets: 112 Meditations to Discover the Mystery Within. Osho, 1931–1990* (1st updated and rev. U.S. ed.), Osho Rajneesh. St. Martin's Press, 2010

23   Pamela Dussault Runtagh describes the concept of vibration as follows: "The higher the frequency of your energy or vibration, the lighter you feel in your physical, emotional, and mental bodies. You experience greater personal power, clarity, peace, love, and joy. You have little, if any, discomfort or pain in your physical body, and your emotions are easily dealt with" ('The Benefits of Being in a Higher Vibration', on HuffPost at https://www.huffpost.com/entry/positive-energy_b_1715767?). People who practise meditation and other healing modalities have been measured to have higher vibrations than most people; see https://www.reiki.org/articles/auras-and-chakras.

24   *Let's Eat Right To Keep Fit*, Adelle Davis, Harcourt, Brace and Company, Inc. 1954, p. 28.

25   *Eat Right 4 Your Type*, Peter D'Adamo with Catherine Whitney, G.P. Putnam's Sons, 1996.

26   *The Body Ecology Diet: Recovering Your Health and Rebuilding Your Immunity*, Donna Gates, Hay House, 2011.

27   *The Pure Cure: A Complete Guide to Freeing Your Life from Dangerous Toxins*, Sharyn Wynters. Soft Skull Press, 2012, p. 27

28   Ibid

29   *Sick Building Syndrome: in Public Buildings and Workplaces*, Abdul-Wahab, Sabah A. (ed.). Springer, 2011, pp. 502, 503

30   https://www.bodyandsoul.com.au/mind-body/wellbeing/negative-ions-are-great-for-your-health/news-story/80565fd02f082d369e7671b230cf908e

31   *Partnering with Nature: The Wild Path to Reconnecting with the Earth,* Catriona MacGregor. Atria Books/Beyond Words, 2010, p. 149

Further Reading

Barefoot Doctor's Handbook for the Urban Warrior: A Spiritual Survival Guide, The Barefoot Doctor, Piatkus Books, 1998.

Classical 5 Element Acupuncture, Vol. 3: The Five Elements and the Officials, J. R. Worsley, Worsley Inc. (1998).

Ecstatic Sex: A Guide to the Pleasures of Tantra, Ma Ananda Sarita and Swami Anand Geho (2003)

Return of the Urban Warrior: High-Speed Spirituality for People on the Run, The Barefoot Doctor, Thorsons (2001)

Sweat Your Prayers: Movement as Spiritual Practice, Gabrielle Roth, Gill Books (1999)

The Tao of Health, Sex and Longevity, Daniel P Reid, Prentice Hall (1989)

Traditional Acupuncture: The Law of the Five Elements, Dianne M. Connolly, Traditional Acupuncture Institute U.S. (1994).

Richard's Wise Words

'The connection with our heart is our connection with spirit,
it's home, our home, look into the eyes of another and all shall
truly be revealed, the lights shall come on and the spirit shall
occupy one's body, the truth will be seen and magic will be the
norm, faith will become reality and the crash and burn of life
and love will sparkle an effervescent glory unto the heart
and soul of the dance of existence itself.
I am alive, I shall not be denied...'

'Energy is constantly, moment to moment,
seeking to find balance, to find its highest potential.'

'It's not about trying to change you into something else, just make you more of who you really are.'

The beginning…

 **Matador**

For exclusive discounts on Matador titles,
sign up to our occasional newsletter at
troubador.co.uk/bookshop